Drawing Close To God In A Time Of Crisis

Finding God In The Storm

David R. Hibbert

Destiny Media Productions
Brossard, Quebec, Canada

Drawing Close To God In A Time Of Crisis
Finding God In The Storm

Destiny Media Productions
P.O. Box 30504
Brossard, Quebec, Canada J4Z 3R6
(450) 676-6944
Email: resource@destinyresource.ca.
Website: www.destinyresource.ca.

ISBN Paperback Book: 978-1-988738-67-3.
ISBN Digital Book: 978-1-988738-68-0.

Cover design by Melissa Baker-Nguyen of Lost Bumblebee Graphics. Address inquiries to lostbumblebee@gmail.com.

STRONGS – All Greek and Hebrew definitions marked “STRONGS” are taken from “Strong's Exhaustive Concordance of the Bible”, generally known as Strong's

Concordance. It is a concordance of the King James Bible (KJV) that was constructed under the direction of Dr. James Strong (1822–1894) and first published in 1890. This concordance is in the public domain (no copyright).

Table Of Contents

Knowing What To Do In A Crisis

Part 1 – Knowing What To Do

You Are In A Season Of Change.

Whenever we are in the midst of a crisis, we are in a season of change. Whenever we face a crisis, things change. Some things change for just a season, and some things change forever.

1. 9/11.

When we experienced what has become known as 9/11, on September 11, 2001, some things changed for a season. Flights were grounded for a season, borders were closed for a season, and people did not travel for a season.

But some other things changed forever. Security measures in airports have changed forever. The way that world governments work together concerning terrorism, has changed forever. Many laws have changed forever.

2. COVID-19.

Now that we are in the midst of another crisis, known as the COVID-19 pandemic, some things will change for a season. Borders are closed for a season. Flights are limited for a season. Physical distancing is in effect for a season. Large public gatherings are being banned for a season.

But other things will be changed forever. Social hygiene habits will be changed forever. The workplace space will be changed forever. Business and relational interaction will be changed forever. Many church ministry strategies will be changed forever.

3. **Every Crisis Changes Things.**

At this point, we do not even know all of the things in society that are going to change.

Every crisis, whether big or small, whether global or local, or even personal – changes things. Some things change for a season, and some things change forever.

Knowing What To Do

1. **Maintaining Healthy Relationships.**

Putting aside for a moment – the world, our society, our workplace, our homeplace, and our social circles – including our church – the question to be asked is ... how do WE, personally, need to respond? In the midst of a crisis, what do WE personally need to do?

In **1 Chronicles 12**, David was facing a crisis. Saul was trying to kill him, and David was banished to Ziklag, hiding from Saul. You could say that David was in a type of self-isolation.

But then slowly, people started to come to David, to encourage him and support him. And David told them that as long as they came in peace, he would welcome them. You see, we all need to maintain healthy relationships, even in a time of isolation.

2. **Understanding The Times.**

And in the middle of David's crisis, the Bible pointed out a special group of people – the people of the tribe of Issachar.

1 Chronicles 12:32, LITV – *(32) And of the sons of Issachar, having understanding of the times, to know what*

Israel should do. Their heads were two hundred, and all their brothers were at their command.

The Bible says three specific things about the sons of Issachar.

They Contributed 200 Leaders.

FIRST, this group contributed 200 heads or chiefs or leaders to the cause of David. Other groups provided brave warriors, but this group provided leaders.

Why did they have so many leaders to contribute to David's cause? Because of the SECOND thing that the Bible says about this group.

They Had Understanding Of The Times.

The Bible says that they had understanding of the times. They looked around them, they considered the situation, and they understood exactly what was happening, and the consequences of what was happening.

They Knew What To Do.

And as a result, the Bible says a THIRD thing about this group. It says that they KNEW what Israel should do. They knew what THEY should do, and they knew what was best for those around them. They knew the best course of action – the best strategy, for themselves and for those around them.

Now, what does this have to do with the crisis we are going through right now?

3. Releasing (Letting Go) And Embracing.

Every crisis forces us into a season of transition. And every transition means that we must let go of some things – we must RELEASE a number of OLD things, and we must EMBRACE a number of NEW things.

And so, NOW is the time to be like the people of Issachar. We need to look around us, discern what is going on, with the help of the Holy Spirit, and then ask God for wisdom so that we know what we should do about it. We need to know what OLD things to RELEASE, and what NEW things to EMBRACE.

And if we will do that, we will have the potential to become leaders, to help others during THEIR time of crisis.

We may become the leaders in our communities, we may become the leaders in our business, we may become the leaders in our churches, we may become the leaders of some group of people. And – if nothing else, we must at least become the leaders of our own lives, rather than being driven by the advice or demands of others, and by the circumstances around us.

As one person said, we need to **re-evaluate**, **re-align**, and **re-start** our lives, our habits, our ministries, our business, and even our churches. Or, as another person said, first we need to do a **check-up**, then we need to do a **tune-up**, and then we need to **step-up**.

Prayer.

"Lord, we ask You to help us **re-evaluate** our lives, and show us what is unhealthy in our lives, that needs to be released. Lord, help us to **re-align** ourselves with what You tell us is best for our lives, and help us to **re-start** our lives on a healthier path, with more healthy life-habits."

"Help us to do an honest self-**check-up** to discover what needs to be changed in our lives, help us to **tune-up** those things that need adjustment, and help us to **step up** and begin to go forward with new discipline, new courage, and a new and complete trust in You."

Assignment.

1. Spend some time alone with God and ask Him to show you the present condition of your life. Ask Him to show you both the healthy things, as well as the unhealthy things.

2. Write down those things that must be released, and one by one, pray and let go of them.

3. Write down those things that must be embraced and re-aligned with God's purposes, and one by one, pray and embrace them.

4. Write down God's strategy for re-starting your life on a healthier path and go forward with new courage and determination.

Part 2 – Caring For Our Soul

1. The Front Stage and Back Stage Of Our Life.

Lance Witt[1], an American Bible teacher, said that our lives are like unfolding dramas on the stage of life. But, in any theatre, there are actually two stages – the front stage and the backstage. The same is true in our lives – we all have a front stage, and a backstage.

The Front Stage – What I Do.

We all have a front stage, where the public sees us. It is where we are noticed, where the spotlight is on us, and where people applaud and affirm us. The front stage is all about "doing" – what I do.

The Back Stage – Who I Am.

We also all have a backstage. It is our private world, that is unseen by most people. The audience is not allowed into our backstage. It is dark, and usually messy. The backstage is all about "being" – who I am.

2. Work On Our Backstage.

During this time of crisis, I have heard many people tell me that God is speaking to them to work on their backstage. No, they have not used those particular words, but that IS what they are saying.

They are saying that they feel God is wanting them to draw close to Him, to spend time with Him, and to let Him remove every obstacle from their lives, and to liberate them from fears, phobias, insecurities, and guilt and

---

[1] Soul Care: The Most Valuable Resource For Great Preaching – Lance Witt, Feb. 27, 2020, Replenish Ministries.

shame. And yes, to also purify them and empower them and re-tune them for the next season ahead.

So, in one sense, we are like the people of Issachar that I talked about. We have understood the season we are in, and we are agreed on what to do. During this time of crisis and isolation, we need to draw close to God.

However, when I ask people what they are doing – what strategy they are using in order to draw close to God, most do not have an answer to give me – they do not have a strategy on how they will draw close to God.

They are unsure of specifically what to do, how to proceed, or what plan to implement to draw close to God. And so, for many, this time of isolation is more of a time of regret and frustration, than a time of renewal and fulfillment.

3. **We Must Develop A Strategy.**

There are some people who are so used to the secret place of Psalm 91 – they are so used to drawing close to God, that developing a strategy to draw close to God seems so simple to them. People like prophetic intercessors have an amazing ability to know how to draw close to God, no matter what is going on around them.

However, for many of us, developing a strategy to draw close to God may be quite foreign to us.

I do not say that to criticize anyone. I say that for those of us who may be struggling, so that we will be encouraged to continue to attempt to develop a plan. God is faithful, and He has made us some amazing promises to inspire us.

James 4:8, NIV – *(8) Draw near to God and He will draw near to you.*

2 Chronicles 15:2, NIV – *(2) "... If you seek Him, He will be found by you ..."*

God promises that if we will attempt to draw near to God, He will draw near to us. In fact, He will begin to move closer to us as soon as we even attempt to move closer to Him.

So, we need to be like the people of Issachar. We need to discern and understand the season we are in, and many have rightly done that. But we also need to know what to do and develop a plan or strategy to do it.

Let us look at David the Psalmist for a moment and allow him to be an inspiration for us.

4. David's Response To Crisis.

David the Psalmist seemed to go through so many trials in his life – his life seemed to be almost always in crisis. But He also seemed to most often know what to do in the midst of every crisis.

In Psalm 42, David was in another time of crisis. And as a result, he was again in a time of isolation.

Psalm 42:4, NIV – *(4) These things I remember as I pour out my soul: how I used to go with the multitude, leading the procession to the house of God, with shouts of joy and thanksgiving among the festive throng.*

He used to be with the multitude, he used to go with others to the house of God, he used to enjoy a time of corporate worship. But now, he was isolated, because of a crisis.

So, what did he pray?

Psalm 42:5-7, NIV – *(5) Why are you downcast, O my soul? Why so disturbed within me? Put your hope in God, for I will yet praise him, my Savior and (6) my God. My soul is downcast within me; therefore I will remember you from the land of the Jordan, the heights of Hermon — from Mount Mizar. (7) Deep calls to deep in the roar of your waterfalls ...*

David did not try to blame others for his problems. And he did not allow himself to focus on his crisis – on his circumstances.

Instead, he ministered to his soul – he talked to his soul, because he realized that no matter what was going on **AROUND** him, it was what was going on **IN** him that was the more important issue.

And so, during his time of crisis, he decided to do four things.

Focus His Hope In God – *"Put your hope in God".*

First, he directed his soul to hope in God. He decided that it was imperative that he focus his hope and trust in God. And so, he took authority over his soul and commanded it, *"put your hope in God".*

Intensify His Worship Of God – *"I will yet praise him".*

Second, he intensified his worship of God. No matter what was going on around him, David decided *"I will yet praise Him".*

Remember The Goodness Of God - *"... I will remember You ..."*

Third, rather than focus on the bad things going on around him, He would focus on the goodness of God. He said, *"... I will remember You ..."*

He would remember those days in Jordan, where he had experienced the goodness, and faithfulness, and mercy of God. He remembered those times on mount Hermon, where he had experienced, with joy, the presence of God.

Deepen His Intimacy With God - *"deep calls to deep".*

Fourth, David choose to go deep with God. He said, *"deep calls to deep".* David decided that during his time of crisis, he would go even deeper in his intimacy with God.

5. **Don't Give Up!**

This was a time of great struggle in David's personal life. So, David had to keep renewing his commitment to go deeper in his relationship with God.

Psalm 42:11, NIV – *(11) Why are you downcast, O my soul? Why so disturbed within me? Put your hope in God, for I will yet praise him, my Savior and my God.*

Psalm 43:5, NIV – *(5) Why are you downcast, O my soul? Why so disturbed within me? Put your hope in God, for I will yet praise him, my Savior and my God.*

David, like the people of Issachar, understood the times he was in. He understood what was going on AROUND him, and IN him. And so, he developed a strategy, to draw close to God in his time of crisis.

In the next number of lessons, I want to give you some guidance, and an example of how we can all develop a strategy to, "Draw Close To God In A Time Of Crisis".

Prayer.

"Lord, help us to be like the people of Issachar. Help us to discern the times that we are in, help us to know what we personally should do, help us to develop a personal strategy for our life, and then give us the courage and discipline to do it."

Assignment

1. Read Psalm 42:5-7 through several times.

2. Focus Your Hope In God

   Take authority over your soul and commanded it to put its hope in God.

3. Intensify Your Worship Of God

   Spend some time every day, just praising God for what He has done, and worshipping God for Who He is.

4. Remember The Goodness Of God

   Start a journal and keep a record of when and how God has been good to you. As you read through it, God will remind you of even more times that you can add to your journal. Use this journal to encourage yourself, whenever you are feeling discouraged or alone.

5. Deepen Your Intimacy With God.

   Begin to go deeper with God, as you spend time each day with Him. Spend time in His presence every day, quiet before Him, and just let Him love you, and minister to you.

Part 3 – How To Begin Your Journey With God

Begin Your Journey With God.

Now, what if you realize that you need to draw closer to God, but you are not sure about your present relationship with God? What if you are not really sure you are His child? Maybe you have never asked Him into your life before? Or perhaps, you just have doubts about your relationship?

Well, today you can give your life to God, and be sure that you are in a relationship with Him, because He will be your Heavenly Father, and you will be His son or daughter.

The first step in drawing close to God, is to **begin** your journey with God.

John 14:6, NIV - *Jesus answered, "I am the way and the truth and the life. No one comes to the Father except through me.*

If we want to draw close to God – if we want to begin our journey with God – we must go through His Son, Jesus Christ.

Living a life in partnership with God, through His Son Jesus, is the greatest adventure any person can ever experience. How can we make the initial decision to trust Him with our whole life, and begin to live for Him, and with Him? It is as simple as A-B-C-D!

A – Admit.

We **admit** that our lives are completely lost, and that Jesus is indeed the only way to salvation.

Romans 3:23,10, NIV – *(23) for all have sinned and fall short of the glory of God. ... (10) ... "There is no one righteous, not even one".*

John 3:16-18, NIV – *(16) "For God so loved the world that he gave his one and only Son, that whoever believes in him shall not perish but have eternal life. ... (18) Whoever believes in him is not condemned, but whoever does not believe stands condemned already because he has not believed in the name of God's one and only Son.*

Acts 4:12, NIV – *(12) Salvation is found in no one else, for there is no other name under heaven given to men by which we must be saved."*

B – Believe.

We **believe** that Jesus died on the cross for our sins and rose from the dead for our freedom.

John 1:29, NIV – *(29) The next day John saw Jesus coming toward him and said, "Look, the Lamb of God, who takes away the sin of the world!"*

1 Corinthians 15:3-4, NIV – *(3) ... that Christ died for our sins according to the Scriptures, (4) that he was buried, that he was raised on the third day ..."*

John 5:24, NIV – *(24) "I tell you the truth, whoever hears my word and believes him who sent me has eternal life and will not be condemned; he has crossed over from death to life.*

C – Confess.

We **confess** Jesus as our personal Lord and Saviour, the new leader of our lives.

Romans 10:9, NIV – *(9) That if you confess with your mouth, "Jesus is Lord," and believe in your heart that God raised him from the dead, you will be saved.*

John 1:12-13, NIV – *(12) Yet to all who received him, to those who believed in his name, he gave the right to become children of God — (13) children born not of natural descent, nor of human decision or a husband's will, but born of God.*

D – Decide.

We **decide** to follow Jesus daily, and do what He asks of us.

Luke 9:23-24, NIV – *(23) Then he said to them all: "If anyone would come after me, he must deny himself and take up his cross daily and follow me. (24) For whoever wants to save his life will lose it, but whoever loses his life for me will save it.*

Prayer.

We can make those four choices, by saying a prayer something like this:

"Jesus, I realize that I am lost without You, and You are the only way that I can experience freedom from my sins."

"Thank You for dying on the cross to save me from the penalty of sin, and for rising from the dead so that I could be completely free."

"I choose to confess and put my trust in You as my Lord and Savior. I give my whole heart and my whole life to You."

“I ask You to indwell me by Your Holy Spirit, so that I can have Your help to do my best to follow You and please You each and every day.”

“In Jesus’ name I pray. Amen!”

If you have prayed this prayer, write today’s date below the prayer, as a record of your commitment.

Congratulations! You have begun your journey with God. Or perhaps you have just reaffirmed your commitment to Him.

Either way, you can now refuse to entertain any doubts about your relationship with Him. And now, you can move forward and grow in intimacy with your Heavenly Father, as you begin to draw closer to Him.

Let us proceed!

~ 27 ~

Learning To Meditate On God’s Word and His Ways

Part 4 – The Art Of Biblical Meditation

1. David Was Skilled In Biblical Mediation.

Before we can start to really draw close to God in a time of crisis, there is one skill, or one tool, or really – an ART – that we all need to develop and learn to use.

And that is the art of meditation ... **NOT** new age meditation, but Biblical meditation.

We talked last time about how David drew closer to God, every time he faced a time of crisis. And the way He did that, every time, was by meditating on God and His word.

Psalm 19:14, NIV – *(14) "May the words of my mouth and the meditation of my heart be pleasing in your sight, O LORD, my Rock and my Redeemer."*

Psalm 104:34, NIV – *(34) "May my meditation be pleasing to him, as I rejoice in the LORD."*

Psalm 119:15, NIV – *(15) "I meditate on your precepts and consider your ways."*

Psalm 119:148, NIV – *(148) "My eyes stay open through the watches of the night, that I may meditate on your promises. "*

Psalm 143:5, NIV – *(5) "I remember the days of long ago; I meditate on all your works and consider what your hands have done."*

The secret to David drawing close to God in every crisis, and the secret to David eventually overcoming every crisis, was through his practice of Biblical mediation.

In fact, every successful leader in the Bible practiced Biblical meditation.

2. The Power Of Meditation.

Abraham – A Prosperous Leader

Genesis 24:63, NIV – *(63) "He went out to the field one evening to meditate, and as he looked up, he saw camels approaching."*

Abraham was a great and prosperous leader, who had a regular habit of going off by himself to meditate. It was often that as he meditated, he had encounters with God and angels, and received revelation from the Lord.

Joshua – A Prosperous Leader

Joshua 1:8, NIV – *(8) "Do not let this Book of the Law depart from your mouth; meditate on it day and night, so that you may be careful to do everything written in it. Then you will be prosperous and successful."*

Joshua was a great and prosperous leader, and he challenged the people of Israel to make a regular habit of meditating on God's word. And he told them that if they did, they also would be prosperous.

Any Blessed Person.

Psalm 1:1-3, NIV – *(1) Blessed is the man ... (2) ... his delight is in the law of the LORD, and on his law he meditates day and night. (3) He is like a tree planted by streams of water, which yields its fruit in season and whose leaf does not wither. Whatever he does prospers.*

We are told that ANY person who wants to be blessed and prosperous and steadfast and fruitful, will meditate on God's word.

3. The Focus Of Our Meditation.

What specifically should we meditate on?

God's Word – His Truth.

Psalm 119:15, NIV – *(15) "I meditate on your precepts ...."*

God's precepts are His commands and laws, that were given to keep His people safe, and reveal His Fatherly nature.

God's Ways – His Actions.

Psalm 119:15, NIV – *(15) "I meditate on your precepts and consider your ways."*

God ways are His manners, the way that He relates to His people and to their sinful and broken condition.

God's Promises – His Faithfulness.

Psalm 119:148, NIV – *(148) "... I may meditate on your promises. "*

God's promises are His appointments, His decrees, and hence His promises, that He has made to His people for their benefit.

God's Heart – His Love.

Psalm 48:9, NIV – *(9) "... we meditate on your unfailing love."*

That phrase, unfailing love, includes all of the ways that He manifests His love toward us, including His kindness, His favour, His goodness, and His mercy toward us.

4. How To Meditate.

So ... how do we meditate?

There are a number of different words used in the Bible for the word "Meditate", because there are a number of different aspects and expressions of Biblical meditation, and that is why I called it an art to be learned.

Strong's H1897 (הָגָה [hâgâh]) = "to murmur, to ponder, to imagine, to mutter, to study" (25x).

Strong's H7742 (שׂוּחַ [śûach]) = "to muse pensively, to think carefully about" (1x).

Strong's H7878 (שִׂיחַ [śîyach]) = "to ponder, to converse with oneself out loud, to commune, to complain, to declare, to muse, to pray, to speak, to talk with" (20x).

Strong's H7879 (שִׂיחַ [śîyach]) = "to contemplate, to utter, to babble". (14x).

Strong's H7881 (שִׂיחָה [śîychâh]) = "to reflect, to make devotion" (3x)

Strong's G3191 (μελετάω [meletaō]) = "to revolve in the mind, to imagine" (3x).

So, putting all of these definitions together, how do we mediate?

Study Thoughtfully.

First, we study the word of God and the character of God, and we think about it, so that we can understand what the Bible really says, and not just what someone told us it says.

We study the word and character of God for ourselves, and as we do, God gives us additional revelation into who He is, and what He wants for us.

Speak To Ourselves.

Second, we speak the word of God quietly, to ourselves, and consider it. We ask ourselves questions about what the Bible is trying to tell us personally. And as we do so, God will give us insight into issues in our heart that need to be healed, and thoughts that need to be corrected.

Speak To God.

Third, we take the word of God and speak to God about it. We ask Him what He wants to say to us through His word. We ask Him what He wants to do in our lives through His word. We ask Him what He wants to teach us through His word. And we ask Him how He wants to change us through His word.

Imagine / Picture.

Fourth, we use our sanctified imagination, and we picture what God is trying to say to us.

We picture the events and actions and events in the Bible and see what we can learn from them. We picture God as He moved, and we discover new things about His ways and His heart. And we even picture ourselves in the Bible, interacting with the story.

Contemplate and Reflect.

Fifth, we contemplate and reflect on God's word and God's ways. We don't just read a verse, and rush on to the next one. Instead, we stay on a verse, and reflect on it over and over, until we receive all of the insight and revelation that God has for us in that verse.

And as we do so, we develop new insights about God's heart, His character, and who He really is, and how He wants to bring about transformation in our lives. And as a side benefit, we will actually memorize most verses that we meditate on.

5. The Example of a Cow

The best example in life we have about how to meditate, comes from the example of the cow.

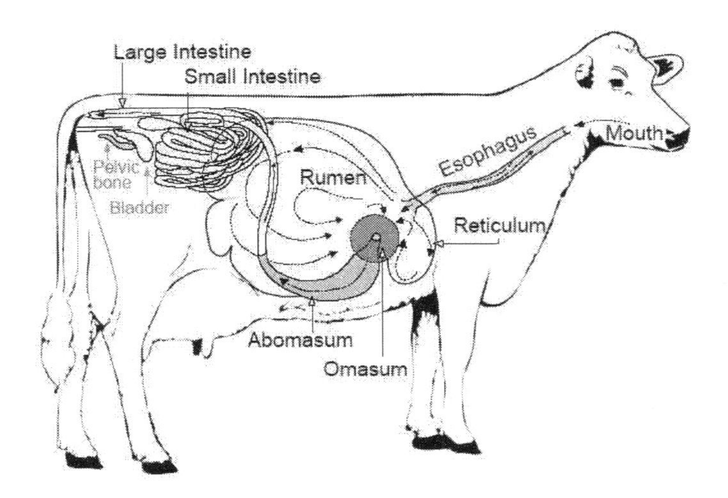

A cow's stomach has four distinct compartments. When a cow chews its "cud", each compartment helps to break down and absorb the food. A cow burps up its cud into its mouth, so that it can keep re-chewing it, and re-swallowing it, over and over, in order to better digest its food.

In the same way, when we meditate, we take the word of God and read it, study it, consider it, speak it, pray it, contemplate and reflect on it, and we turn it over and over again in our mind and heart and spirit. And we keep "chewing" on it until we receive as much revelation or spiritual food from it as we can.

Matthew 4:4, NIV – *(4) "... "Man does not live on bread alone, but on every word that comes from the mouth of God.""*

We don't eat bread by shoving as much of it as we can down our throats. Instead, we eat bread piece by piece by chewing it over and over again, until it has been broken apart, so that it can be easily digested. And God says, "don't just eat bread to live, eat also my word".

So, we treat the word of God as food and nourishment, and we eat and chew on it each and every day.

Prayer.

"Father, help us as we learn how to use Biblical meditation. Help us to meditate on Your word and Your ways, so that we can receive the full revelation that You want us to know, and so that we can come to know Your heart so well, that it becomes easy to draw close to You in a time of crisis."

Reminder: How To Meditate.

1. Study Thoughtfully.
2. Speak To Ourselves.
3. Speak To God.
4. Imagine / Picture.
5. Contemplate and Reflect.

Assignment.

1. Begin today, to practice and develop the art of Biblical meditation, using the principles outlined in this lesson.

2. Keep a record of the insights that God gives you, as you meditate.

Part 5 – An Example Of Biblical Meditation

Learning To Meditate.

Before we look more deeply at how to draw close to God in a time of crisis, lets first look at an example of how to use Biblical meditation. Let us use Psalm 1:1-6 as an example.

Psalm 1:1-6, NIV – *(1) Blessed is the man who does not walk in the counsel of the wicked or stand in the way of sinners or sit in the seat of mockers. (2) But his delight is in the law of the LORD, and on his law he meditates day and night. (3) He is like a tree planted by streams of water, which yields its fruit in season and whose leaf does not wither. Whatever he does prospers. (4) Not so the wicked! They are like chaff that the wind blows away. (5) Therefore the wicked will not stand in the judgment, nor sinners in the assembly of the righteous. (6) For the LORD watches over the way of the righteous, but the way of the wicked will perish.*

Now, just to help you in your Bible study and meditation, I encourage you to download the **free** Bible study software, called "e-sword". You can download it from https://www.e-sword.net. It is available for a PC or Mac computer, and also for an iPad or iPhone.

For an android device, you will have to use the **free** alternative: "MySword". It is available from: https://www.mysword.info/.

So, let us learn to meditate with Psalm 1:1-3.

1. **Blessed is the man (vs. 1).**

   Think about that word "blessed".

The word blessed (Strong's H835 = אֶשֶׁר ['esher]) means "to be blessed, to be happy, to be full of joy, to prosper, to go forward on a level path".

So, ask yourself what it looks like for you, personally, to be blessed – to be so happy that you are overflowing with joy.

What would it look like to be prosperous in every area of your life? Prosperous in your health, prosperous in your emotions, prosperous in your thought life, prosperous in your relationships, prosperous in your finances, and prosperous in your spiritual life.

What would it look like if you walked on a level path your whole life, never stumbling due to fear, anxiety or worry, and never getting tripped up by deception or the schemes or opinions of men?

2. **Who Does Not (vs. 1):**

Walk In The Counsel Of The Wicked.

The word "walk" (Strong's H1980 = הָלַךְ [hâlak]) means "to walk, to behave".

The word "counsel" (Strong's H6098 = עֵצָה ['êtsâh]) means "advice" or "plans".

The word "wicked" (Strong's H7563 = רָשָׁע [râshâʻ]) means "the morally wrong", and therefore, those who DO wrong.

So, picture yourself refusing to follow any advice from people who you know are unethical, or who have questionable practices. See yourself putting your hands over your ears and refusing to listen to them.

What would your life be like if you refused all advice from ungodly people?

Stand In The Way Of Sinners.

The word “stand” (Strong’s H5975 = עָמַד ['âmad]) means “to abide, continue in, dwell in, be established in, remain in”.

The word “way” (Strong’s H1870 = דֶּרֶךְ [derek]) means “a road, a course of life”.

The word “sinners” (Strong’s H2400 = חַטָּא [chaṭṭâ']) means “those accounted as guilty, offenders”.

So, to stand in the way of sinners, means to get pulled into the lifestyle of people who are corrupt. We may get tempted or tricked into a wrong choice, but we must not allow ourselves to adopt a way of life that is corrupt.

So, picture yourself as being tempted, but immediately turn away from those choices, and if need be, to repent for even entertaining the idea. See yourself literally jumping out of anything that you discover is questionable, or unethical. Instead, see yourself living in a manner that always brings blessing and favour to yourself, your family, and others.

Sit In The Seat Of Mockers

The word “sit” (Strong’s H3427 = יָשַׁב [yâshab]) means “to sit down as a judge, to sit quietly, to wait in ambush, to dwell, to remain, to abide”.

The word “seat” (Strong’s H4186 = מוֹשָׁב [môshâb]) means “a seat, a place of abode or dwelling, to stay in a situation”.

The word “mockers” (Strong’s H3887 = לוּץ [lûts]) means “to scoff, to deride, to mock, to scorn”

So to sit in the seat of mockers, means to allow a critical spirit to come into our hearts, so that we make judgments on other people by mocking and scorning them, in an attempt to put them down or cause them to stumble.

So, picture yourself guarding your heart and watching your words. Maybe even picture a special mask on your mouth that filters out every negative word, so that no critical words are coming out of your mouth. Instead, see words of life coming out of your mouth. See your very breath causing things around you to grow and flourish.

3. **His Delight Is In The Law Of The LORD (vs. 2).**

The word “delight” (Strong’s H2656 = חֵפֶץ [chêphets]) means “to find pleasure, to desire, to consider something very valuable”.

The word “law” (Strong’s H8451 = תּוֹרָה [tôrâh]) means “the precepts, the statutes” and especially the first five books of the Bible.

So, to delight in the law of the Lord is to consider God’s word of great value, and something we desire to read and study and enjoy. We find enjoyment in reading it and applying it in our lives.

So, picture yourself sitting down with God’s word, and reading it. Perhaps picture it as light shining into our mind and transforming it. Picture it shining into your heart and healing it. And picture it shining into your very spirit and strengthening it.

4. **On His Law He Meditates Day And Night (vs. 2).**

The word “meditate” used here (Strong’s H1897 = הָגָה [hâgâh]) means “to murmur in pleasure, to ponder, to imagine, to mediate, to speak, to study, to talk”.

The word “day” (Strong’s H3119 = יוֹמָם [yômâm]) means both “in the day” and “daily”.

The word “night” (Strong’s H3915 = לַיִל [layil]) means “away from the day”, and so “at night”.

So, the Bible is encouraging us to make a habit of reflecting on God’s word daily, throughout the day, and even at night.

So, picture yourself rising, and reading a short passage of the Bible. Then picture yourself reflecting on that passage, as you shower, get dressed, eat breakfast, and head off to work. Picture yourself taking time during your work breaks to reflect on that passage again, as an encouragement to yourself.

See yourself on your way home again reflecting on the passage. See yourself after supper sharing your insights with your spouse, or family, or with a friend. And see yourself thanking the Lord for that passage, as you lay down to sleep.

5. **He Is Like A Tree Planted By Streams Of Water (vs. 3).**

The word “tree” (Strong’s H6086 = עֵץ [ʿêts]) means “a firm tree, a piece of strong timber”.

The word “planted” (Strong’s H8362 = שָׁתַל [shâthal]) means “to be transplanted”.

The word “streams” (Strong’s H6388 = פֶּלֶג [peleg]) means “a small channel or tributary of water used for irrigation”.

The word “water” (Strong’s H4325 = מַיִם [mayim]) means “water, juice, water that is filled with life and refreshes and brings life”.

So, if we will take the time to mediate on God's word, not only will we not fall into one of the traps of verse one, we will instead become like a strong and healthy tree.

So, picture yourself as a little tree that bends in the wind. Now picture yourself being taken out of your dry ground and being transplanted into the soil beside an irrigation channel of water.

See yourself draw water from this irrigation channel that was created just for you. See yourself receiving life from that water and becoming stronger and healthier each and every day.

Now see yourself growing and growing, until you are a tall oak tree, able to withstand even gale-force winds.

6. **Which Yields Its Fruit In Season (vs. 3).**

The word "yields" (Strong's H5414 = נָתַן [nâthan]) means "to make, to give, to bestow, to bring forth, to shoot forth".

The word "fruit" (Strong's H6529 = פְּרִי [perîy]) means "fruit, fruitful, reward".

The word "season" (Strong's H6256 = עֵת [ʿêth]) means "time, now and after, continually, throughout the seasons".

So, what happens if we make a habit of meditating on God's word?

Picture yourself growing and shooting forth great fruit. Like with a time-lapse camera, see fruit coming out of your life so greatly, and so speedily, that it literally shoots out of you.

And see that fruit coming forth in every season. In spring, in summer, in fall, and even in winter – see your fruit continuing to flourish.

And see that this fruit is not only a blessing to others, but also a reward that you yourself can eat.

7. And Whose Leaf Does Not Wither (vs. 3).

The word "leaf" (Strong's H5929 = עָלֶה ['âleh]) means "a leaf, foliage".

The word "wither" (Strong's H5034 = נָבֵל [nâbêl]) means "to wilt, to fall away, to fail, to faint, to be foolish, to cause disgrace or dishonour, to fade, to come to nought".

So, the Bible says that if we develop a lifestyle of Biblical meditation, our life and our legacy will never fail. Our life will never cause us disgrace or dishonour or lack of fruit. Instead, we will live a life of continued fruitfulness and blessing.

Picture yourself as that oak tree, always staying strong through every storm, bearing fruit in spring, summer, fall and winter, and still bearing fruit after ten years, twenty years, thirty years, forty years, and even fifty years and more.

8. Whatever He Does Prospers (vs. 3).

The word "whatever" (Strong's H3605 = כֹּל [kôl]) means "the whole, every, all, any, altogether, whatsoever, as many as".

The word "prosper" (Strong's H6743 = צָלַח [tsâlach]) means "to push forward, to break out, to come mightily, to be profitable, to make prosperous".

So, if we develop a lifestyle of Biblical meditation, God's word promises that everything we do, and the whole of our life, will be prosperous. We will keep pushing forward, we will keep breaking through, we will become mighty in our lives, and we will experience ongoing prosperity.

So, picture yourself as that great oak tree, and see your roots spreading, and pushing all stones and structures out of your way. See your tree branches pushing over walls and knocking down every obstacle. And see yourself dropping acorns wherever your branches spread, until you have given birth to a whole forest of oak trees, all healthy, and all prosperous.

Summary.

So that is an example of how to meditate on the word of God, so that you can receive great insight, and great transformation. And that is why Biblical meditation is so important.

Prayer.

"Lord, thank You so much for Biblical mediation. Help me to learn the art of using this tool, so that I can experience all the benefits of meditating on Your word and your ways, including the benefit of drawing close to You in a time of crisis."

Reminder: How To Meditate.

1. Study Thoughtfully.
2. Speak To Ourselves.
3. Speak To God.
4. Imagine / Picture.
5. Contemplate and Reflect.

Assignment:

1. Go back through Psalm 1:1-3, and meditate on these three verses again, and seek God for fresh revelation and insights. Commit to do whatever God shows you.

2. Meditate on the rest of Psalm 1 – verses 4 to 6 – and come up with your own insights, and respond to everything God shows you.

3. Commit to make Biblical meditation a part of your Christian lifestyle.

4. Here are some definitions that may help you:

Verse 4

"Wicked" (Strong's H7563 = רָשָׁע [râshâ']) means "the morally wrong", and therefore, those who DO wrong.

"Chaff" (Strong's H4671 = מֹץ [môts]) means "chaff, threshed loose".

"Wind" (Strong's H7307 = רוּחַ [rûach]) means "wind, breath, blast, tempest".

"Blows away" (Strong's H5086 = נָדַף [nâdaph]) = "to shove asunder, to disperse, to drive away, to be thrust down, to be shaken, to be tossed to and fro".

Verse 5

"Wicked" (Strong's H7563 = רָשָׁע [râshâ']) means "the morally wrong", and therefore, those who DO wrong.

"Stand" (Strong's H6965 = קוּם [qûm]) means "stand, to rise, to abide, continue, make good, to succeed, to remain".

“Judgment” (Strong’s H4941 = מִשְׁפָּט [mishpâṭ]) means “verdict, sentence, formal decree, divine law, justice”.

“Sinners” (Strong’s H2400 = חַטָּא [chaṭṭâ']) means “those accounted as guilty, offenders”.

“Congregation” (Strong’s H5712 = עֵדָה ['êdâh]) means “assembly, congregation, family, crowd, multitude”.

“Righteous” (Strong’s H6662 = צַדִּיק [tsaddîyq]) means “just, lawful, righteous person”.

Verse 6

“Lord” (Strong’s H3068 = יְהֹוָה [yehôvâh]) means “the self-existent or eternal one, the Lord”

“Watches” (Strong’s H3045 = יָדַע [yâda‘]) means “to know by seeing, to observe, to recognize, to acknowledge, to consider”.

“Way” (Strong’s H1870 = דֶּרֶךְ [derek]) means “a road, a course of life”.

“Righteous” (Strong’s H6662 = צַדִּיק [tsaddîyq]) means “just, lawful, righteous person”.

“Wicked” (Strong’s H7563 = רָשָׁע [râshâ‘]) means “the morally wrong”, and therefore, those who DO wrong.

“Perish” (Strong’s H6 = אָבַד ['âbad]) = “wander away, lose oneself, perish, be destroyed, be broken, fail, be undone utterly, to have no way to flee”.

Learning To Draw Close To God

Part 6 – Knowing God As My LORD (YHWH)

A Crisis Look At Psalm 23.

So, now that we are sure that we are a child of God, and we have learned the tool of Biblical mediation, how are we going to draw close to God our Father in a time of crisis?

Psalm 23 has always been a great Psalm to look at during a time of sorrow, or a time of grief. It has brought comfort to hundreds of millions of people over the last 3000 years during times of loss.

But what about comfort during a time of crisis? I want to take a fresh look at Psalm 23 and see how it can help us to draw close to God during a time of crisis.

Psalm 23:1-6, NKJV – *(1) The LORD is my shepherd; I shall not want. (2) He makes me to lie down in green pastures; He leads me beside the still waters. (3) He restores my soul; He leads me in the paths of righteousness For His name's sake. (4) Yea, though I walk through the valley of the shadow of death, I will fear no evil; For You are with me; Your rod and Your staff, they comfort me. (5) You prepare a table before me in the presence of my enemies; You anoint my head with oil; My cup runs over. (6) Surely goodness and mercy shall follow me All the days of my life; And I will dwell in the house of the LORD Forever.*

God My "Lord".

Let us start with the very first phrase.

Verse 1 – *"The* ***Lord*** *is my Shepherd".*

"The Lord".

The Hebrew word translated as "Lord" (Strong's H3068 = יְהֹוָה [yehôvâh]) is called the "Tetragrammaton", which means "four letters". The four letters or four consonants, without vowels, are the Biblical name of our God. The four letters in Hebrew are yodh, he, waw, he. In English, we would write it YHWH, and we usually pronounce it Yahweh, although most people today say Jehovah.

The name "Yahweh" occurs 6521 times in the Old Testament.

Observant Jews revere the name of God so much, that they do not pronounce it "Yahweh". Instead, they replace it with words such as "Adonai" meaning "My Lord", "HaShem" meaning "the Name", or "Hakadosh baruch hu" meaning "the Holy One" or "Blessed Be He"[2].

God The "I Am".

God's name "YHWH" is derived from the Hebrew verb for "to be, to become, to come to pass". That reminds us of Exodus 3.

Exodus 3:13-14, NIV – *(13) Moses said to God, "Suppose I go to the Israelites and say to them, 'The God of your fathers has sent me to you,' and they ask me, 'What is his name?' Then what shall I tell them?" (14) God said to Moses, "I AM WHO I AM. This is what you are to say to the Israelites: 'I AM has sent me to you.'"*

When God said, "I AM", He was using the Hebrew verb "to be".

Now, here are a couple of interesting things about the Hebrew verb "to be".

---

[2]https://en.wikipedia.org/wiki/Tetragrammaton#:~:text=The%20Tetragrammaton%20(%2F%CB%8Ct%C9%9B,%2C%20he%2C%20waw%20and%20he.

FIRST, when God said "I Am", He used the form of the verb that has no tense, so at the exact same time it can mean, "I was, I am, and I will be". Remember in the book of Revelation?

Revelation 4:8, NIV – *(8) ... "Holy, holy, holy is the Lord God Almighty, who was, and is, and is to come."*

SECOND, in Hebrew writing today, the verb "to be" is ONLY used in past tense (I was), or future tense (I will be). It is never used in the present tense (I am), but only in the past or future tense. The present tense "I am" is reserved in the Hebrew language solely for the name of God.

Implications For Us.

So, let us look at some implications of God's name, "Yahweh".

1. Yahweh Is Eternal – He Is Consistent.

The word "YHWH", which is taken from the Hebrew verb "to be" with one more letter added, means "self-existent one, eternal one". The name "Yahweh" speaks of the eternal nature of God – God the self-existent one – God the one who always is.

So, God has always existed, and He always will exist. And since He was not created, nothing created can affect Him.

Genesis 21:33, NIV – *(33) Abraham planted a tamarisk tree in Beersheba, and there he called upon the name of the LORD [Yahweh], the Eternal God.*

God is the Eternal God. He has always existed, and He always will exist, and He will never change.

Malachi 3:6, NIV – *(6) "I the LORD do not change."*

So, when we draw close to Yahweh during a time of crisis, we can know that He is always present, and His love and compassion and mercy will NEVER change.

His arms of love **WERE** always open, His arms of love **ARE** always open, and His arms of love **WILL** always be open. He always **HAS BEEN** merciful, He **IS** merciful, and He always **WILL BE** merciful.

2. Yahweh Is Relational – He Keeps His Promises.

Second, Yahweh is the covenant-keeping name of God[3].

When the creative aspect of God was recorded in Genesis 1, the name Elohim was used for God. The word "Elohiym" (Strongs H430 = אֱלֹהִים ['ĕlôhîym]) is a plural word, that means "supreme God", "exceeding God", or "the plural God", which is only reasonable since God exists as a Trinity.

However, any time that God is mentioned in terms of a relationship with humanity, the name "Yahweh" is always used.

So when we draw close to Yahweh during a time of crisis, we can know we are approaching a God of relationship, we are approaching a God Who desires to confirm and deepen His relationship with us, and a God Who keeps His promises to us.

Leviticus 26:12, NIV – *(12) "I will walk among you and be your God, and you will be my people."*

[3] https://www.blueletterbible.org/faq/don_stewart/don_stewart_1305.cfm

1 Peter 2:9, NIV – *(9) "But you are a chosen people, a royal priesthood, a holy nation, a people belonging to God ... "*

We do not have to be afraid of drawing near to God. We do not have to be afraid that He is going to reject us. We do not have to be afraid that He is going to leave us or forsake us. God has declared that we are His covenant people, and He will always keep His covenant to us.

So, when we draw near to Yahweh God, especially in a time of crisis, we are approaching our covenant-keeping God.

3. Yahweh Is Ever Present – He Is Always With Us.

Third, as I said, when God said "I Am", He used the form of the verb without any tense, so He was saying, "I was, I am, and I will be". That is our God!

Revelation 1:8, NIV – *(8) "I am the Alpha and the Omega," says the Lord God, "who is, and who was, and who is to come, the Almighty."*

God is eternal and cannot be influenced by time, because He is outside of time. But since God is outside of time, no matter what time it is, He is always in the present.

So, when God relates to us, He is always the "I am", and never the "I was", or "I will be".

When we draw near to God in a time of crisis, we never have to wonder where God is. God is **ALWAYS** present, God is always **IN** the present, and God is always in **OUR** present.

We never have to ask, "God, in the middle of this crisis, where ARE You?" We never have to ask, "God, in this moment of trial, where ARE You?" We never have to ask, "God, when I was just a child, and I went through that traumatic event, where WERE You?" And we never have to ask, "God, when this crisis is over, things will still be pretty fearful. Where WILL YOU BE?"

His answer will always be the same. "When you were just a child, I AM with You, right beside you. In the middle of this crisis, I AM with You, right beside you. And in the months ahead, during your future uncertainty, I AM with You, right beside you."

So, as we draw near to God during this time of crisis, we start by taking some time to reflect on who God is that we are drawing close to. He is Yahweh, He is the eternal God, and does not change. He is Yahweh, He is the covenant-keeping God, and He will never reject us. And He is Yahweh, He is the Great I AM, always present, and always IN the present, in every situation.

Prayer.

"Father, as I draw close to You, give me confidence that You are the Eternal God, that You do not change, and that Your love for me is always constant. Father, give me confidence that You are the Covenant-keeping God, and all of Your promises to me are still true. And Father, give me confidence that You are the great I Am, always present, and always IN the present, with me."

Reminder: How To Meditate.

1. Study Thoughtfully.
2. Speak To Ourselves.
3. Speak To God.
4. Imagine / Picture.
5. Contemplate and Reflect.

Assignment.

1. For the next number of days, take time every day to mediate on God as "YHWH", the God who is "I am".

2. Ask Him to reveal to you different aspects of the fact that:

   - Yahweh Is Eternal – He Is Consistent.
   - Yahweh Is Relational – He Keeps His Promises.
   - Yahweh Is Ever Present – He Is Always With Us.

3. Record any insights God gives you and meditate on them.

Part 7 – Knowing God As My Shepherd

A Crisis Look At Psalm 23.

We are looking at Psalm 23, to help us learn how we can draw closer to God during a time of crisis.

Psalm 23:1-6, NKJV – *(1) The LORD is my shepherd; I shall not want. (2) He makes me to lie down in green pastures; He leads me beside the still waters. (3) He restores my soul; He leads me in the paths of righteousness For His name's sake. (4) Yea, though I walk through the valley of the shadow of death, I will fear no evil; For You are with me; Your rod and Your staff, they comfort me. (5) You prepare a table before me in the presence of my enemies; You anoint my head with oil; My cup runs over. (6) Surely goodness and mercy shall follow me All the days of my life; And I will dwell in the house of the LORD Forever.*

God My Shepherd.

Let us continue looking at verse 1 – *"The Lord is **<u>my Shepherd</u>**".*

The word "Shepherd" (Strongs H7462 = רָעָה [râ'âh]) means "to tend a flock, to cause to graze, to associate with a friend, to be a companion".

So, let us look at this definition in more detail.

1. **God Cares For Us.**

   The word Shepherd means "to tend a flock". The word "tend" means "to care for".

   We are God's flock, His sheep, and so God wants to care for us.

Psalm 100:3, NIV – *(3) Know that the LORD is God. It is he who made us, and we are his; we are his people, the sheep of his pasture.*

So, when we draw near to God, we are drawing near to someone who already cares for us. He wants to help us in the way that is best for us, and He always has our best interests at heart.

Nahum 1:7, NIV – *(7) The LORD is good, a refuge in times of trouble. He cares for those who trust in him.*

God is good, He cares for us all. But He can only GIVE care to those who trust in Him, because when we do not trust in Him, we hinder his ability to care for us.

Ephesians 5:29-30, NIV – *(29) After all, no one ever hated his own body, but he feeds and cares for it, just as Christ does the church — (30) for we are members of his body.*

God cares for us, as much as, and even **more** than we care for our own body. As our Shepherd, He cares for us.

1 Peter 5:7, NIV – *(7) Cast all your anxiety on him because he cares for you.*

We have an open invitation from our Shepherd, to cast all of our anxiety and worries and fears on Him, and allow Him to care for all of those things – because He cares for us.

2. God Feeds Us.

The word “Shepherd” also means “to cause to graze”. The word “graze” means “to feed”.

Our Shepherd does not want us to starve, He wants us to eat and be in health – physically, spiritually, emotionally, intellectually, and relationally.

He desires to feed us with what is best for us.

Luke 12:24, NIV – *(24) Consider the ravens: They do not sow or reap, they have no storeroom or barn; yet God feeds them. And how much more valuable you are than birds!*

Our Shepherd wants to care for all of our physical and material needs. But He also wants to care for all of our spiritual and emotional needs.

Matthew 4:4, NIV – *(4) Jesus answered, "It is written: 'Man does not live on bread alone, but on every word that comes from the mouth of God.'"*

Our Shepherd wants us to feed on His word, and also on His very life.

John 6:57-58, NIV – *(57) Just as the living Father sent me and I live because of the Father, so the one who feeds on me will live because of me. (58) This is the bread that came down from heaven. Your forefathers ate manna and died, but he who feeds on this bread will live forever."*

So, let us go beyond **reading** His Word, the Bible, and learn how to actually **feed** on it, for life and nourishment. And let us go beyond **enjoying** His presence, and learn how to actually **feed** on His presence, and receive life from Him.

He is our Shepherd, and He wants to feed us with His word, and His life.

3. God Befriends Us.

The word "Shepherd" also means "to associate with a friend". Our Shepherd wants to befriend us, and then treat us as a friend, and spend time with us.

John 15:13-15, NIV – *(13) Greater love has no one than this, that he lay down his life for his friends. (14) You are my friends if you do what I command. (15) I no longer call you servants, because a servant does not know his master's business. Instead, I have called you friends, for everything that I learned from my Father I have made known to you.*

During our time of crisis, our Shepherd wants us to go beyond being a believer – a convert – someone who believes in Jesus. He wants us to go beyond being a disciple – a student of our Great Teacher. He wants us to go beyond being a servant – someone who does our Master's will. He wants us to be His friend.

He wants us to spend time with Him, and to learn how to be His friend, so that He can make everything He knows, known to us, including His deep love for us.

4. God Dwells With Us.

The word "Shepherd" also means to be a "companion". A companion does not just visit – a companion stays with us.

In the Old Testament, God made a covenant with His people, to never leave them, even during times of crisis.

Deuteronomy 31:8, NIV – *(8) The LORD himself goes before you and will be with you; he will never leave you nor forsake you. Do not be afraid; do not be discouraged."*

In the New Testament, our Shepherd Jesus renewed His promise to His people.

Matthew 28:20, NIV – *"... And surely I am with you always, to the very end of the age."*

How can Jesus keep His promise to us?

John 14:16-17, NIV – *(16) And I will ask the Father, and he will give you another Counselor to be with you forever — (17) the Spirit of truth. ... you know him, for he lives with you and will be in you.*

When Jesus ascended into heaven, He sent to each one of us, the eternal Holy Spirit, to abide WITH us, and IN us forever. So, we now have our Shepherd as an eternal companion through the indwelling Holy Spirit. And He is indeed, always with us.

5. God Pastors Us.

The word "Shepherd" is also translated as "pastor" in the New Testament.

1 Peter 2:25, NIV – *(25) For you were like sheep going astray, but now you have returned to the Shepherd [pastor] and Overseer of your souls.*

The creator of the universe, the eternal one, is our personal pastor! Think of the very best pastor that you have ever had in your life. Now consider this:

The good news is that every Christian already has an even much better pastor. They have the perfect pastor, who desperately wants to lead us and guide us and care for us, if we would just take the time to get to know Him and let Him pastor us.

Summary.

During this, or any time of crisis, let us get to know God as Shepherd, and learn how to let Him care for us, feed us, befriend us, dwell with us, and pastor us.

Prayer.

"Father, teach me how to relate to you as my Shepherd. Help me to trust You, so that You can care for me. Teach me how to let You feed me. Help me to open my heart to You completely, so that You can relate to me as a friend. Help me to know and feel Your presence with me, each and every day, and help me to seek You as my pastor, the one who cares for my soul."

Reminder: How To Meditate.

1. Study Thoughtfully.
2. Speak To Ourselves.
3. Speak To God.
4. Imagine / Picture.
5. Contemplate and Reflect.

Assignment.

1. For the next number of days, take time every day to mediate on God as your "Shepherd".

2. Ask Him to reveal to you different aspects of the fact that:

   - He cares for you.
   - He feeds you.
   - He befriends you.
   - He dwells with you.
   - He pastors you.

3. Record any insights God gives you and meditate on them.

Part 8 – Knowing God As My Provider

A Crisis Look At Psalm 23.

We are looking at Psalm 23, to help us learn how we can draw closer to God during a time of crisis.

Psalm 23:1-6, NKJV – *(1) The LORD is my shepherd; I shall not want. (2) He makes me to lie down in green pastures; He leads me beside the still waters. (3) He restores my soul; He leads me in the paths of righteousness For His name's sake. (4) Yea, though I walk through the valley of the shadow of death, I will fear no evil; For You are with me; Your rod and Your staff, they comfort me. (5) You prepare a table before me in the presence of my enemies; You anoint my head with oil; My cup runs over. (6) Surely goodness and mercy shall follow me All the days of my life; And I will dwell in the house of the LORD Forever.*

My Provider.

Let us look at the second part of verse 1 – *"I shall not want".*

The word "want" (Strong's H2637 = חָסֵר [châsêr]) means "to lack or be in want, to fail, to lessen or decrease or be made lower".

So, let us look at these three definitions in more detail.

1. **We Shall Not Lack Or Be In Want.**

   Psalm 23 says that since the Lord is our Shepherd, we shall not lack or be in want.

   Why? Because God is our provider. God has promised to provide for us, everything that we truly need to do His will on this earth.

Genesis 22:14, NIV – *(14) So Abraham called that place The LORD Will Provide. And to this day it is said, "On the mountain of the LORD it will be provided."*

When Abraham was at his lowest, most desperate moment, as he stood over the sacrificial altar with his son Isaac laying on it, the Lord provided a sacrificial lamb at just the right time.

And when we are in a place of crisis, the Lord will provide, at just the right time, and we will not lack anything that we need.

What if our crisis is a crisis of **temptation**?

1 Corinthians 10:13, NIV – *(13) No temptation has seized you except what is common to man. And God is faithful; he will not let you be tempted beyond what you can bear. But when you are tempted, he will also provide a way out so that you can stand up under it.*

If we stand firm, God will come through, and give us exactly what we need to overcome every temptation.

What if our crisis is because we need **spiritual resources**?

1 Corinthians 1:7, NIV – *(7) Therefore you do not lack any spiritual gift as you eagerly wait for our Lord Jesus Christ to be revealed.*

If we need any spiritual resources, God says that He has already given them to us, and all we have to do is step out in faith and receive them and use them.

What if our crisis is due to a **material need**?

Luke 22:35, NIV – *(35) Then Jesus asked them, "When I sent you without purse, bag or sandals, did you lack anything?" "Nothing," they answered.*

Even when we have nothing at all, because we are His children who are doing His will, we will still not lack anything.

So, whether our need is physical, or spiritual, or material, or whatever, God WILL provide, because God is our provider, and so we shall not lack or be in want.

2. We Shall Not Fail.

Psalm 23:1 also says that since the Lord is our Shepherd, we shall not fail. Why? Because God is our provider, and He will give us what we need so that we can succeed.

Genesis 39:23, NIV – *(23) The warden paid no attention to anything under Joseph's care, because the LORD was with Joseph and gave him success in whatever he did.*

The Lord was with Joseph and gave Him success in whatever He did. And since the Lord is with us, we will experience success and not failure.

2 Chronicles 26:5, NIV – *(5) He [Uzziah] sought God during the days of Zechariah, who instructed him in the fear of God. As long as he sought the LORD, God gave him success.*

Uzziah was only 16 years old when he became King. But as long as he sought the Lord, the Lord gave him success.

Age or intelligence or social or economic status does not matter. If the Lord is with us, we will have success.

1 Chronicles 22:13, NIV – (*13) Then you will have success if you are careful to observe the decrees and laws that the LORD gave Moses for Israel. Be strong and courageous. Do not be afraid or discouraged.*

God promises us that we will not fail, but instead, we will have success, if we follow His decrees and laws.

1 Chronicles 28:20, NIV – *(20) "David also said to Solomon his son, "Be strong and courageous, and do the work. Do not be afraid or discouraged, for the LORD God, my God, is with you. He will not fail you or forsake you ...".*

Why will we not fail? -- Because God will not fail us! And so, no matter what comes against us, we can experience success.

3. We Shall Not Lessen Or Decrease Or Be Made Lower.

Psalm 23 verse one also says that since the Lord is our Shepherd, we shall not "lessen or decrease or be made lower". Why? Because God is our provider, and He will cause us to increase, and not to decrease.

Genesis 1:28, NIV – *(28) God blessed them and said to them, "Be fruitful and increase in number; fill the earth and subdue it."*

Both those words "fruitful" and "increase" are words of growth, increase and abundance. They are not just talking about having children and increasing the population. They are talking about fruitfulness and increase in every part of our lives. God's will for our lives is increase, not decrease.

Deuteronomy 30:16, NIV – *(16) For I command you today to love the LORD your God, to walk in his ways, and to keep his commands, decrees and laws; then you will live and increase, and the LORD your God will bless you in the land you are entering to possess.*

God promises that if we obey His commands and do His will, we will have life, increase, and the blessing of God. God word is a word of increase. God's Kingdom is a kingdom of increase. And so, when we do His word and His will, and serve His kingdom, we will experience increase.

2 Corinthians 9:10, NIV – *(10) Now he who supplies seed to the sower and bread for food will also supply and increase your store of seed and will enlarge the harvest of your righteousness.*

God so much wants us to increase, that He will actually supply or give us "seed" – the resources that we need to do His will, and then He will increase the amount of our seed, and then He will be actively working with us to enlarge our harvest – the fruit of our labour.

1 Peter 5:6, NIV – *(6) Humble yourselves, therefore, under God's mighty hand, that he may lift you up in due time.*

No matter what the situation, God does not want us to be brought down. If we walk in humility before Him and trust Him, He promises that in every situation, He will lift us up to the place that we need to be.

Prayer.

"Father, help me to trust You as my provider, so that I will never be in want, or lack anything. Help me to obey You, so that I shall never fail in what I do for You. And help me to walk in Your ways, so that I may always increase, and never decrease. And as I live humbly before you, thank You that You will always lift me up."

"Thank You, in Jesus' name. Amen!"

Reminder: How To Meditate:

1. Study Thoughtfully.
2. Speak To Ourselves.
3. Speak To God.
4. Imagine / Picture.
5. Contemplate and Reflect.

Assignment.

1. For the next number of days, take time every day to mediate on God as your "Provider".

2. Ask Him to reveal to you different aspects of the fact that, since He is your Provider:

    - You shall not lack or be in want.
    - You shall not fail.
    - You shall not lessen or decrease or be made lower.

3. Record any insights God gives you and meditate on them.

4. Personalize and declare these three statements over your life each and every day, and visualize these three statements to be true in your own life, until your faith grows strong and you are able to live them.

Part 9 – Knowing God As My Rest-Giver.

A Crisis Look At Psalm 23.

We are looking at Psalm 23, to help us learn how we can draw closer to God during a time of crisis.

Psalm 23:1-6, NKJV – *(1) The LORD is my shepherd; I shall not want. (2) He makes me to lie down in green pastures; He leads me beside the still waters. (3) He restores my soul; He leads me in the paths of righteousness For His name's sake. (4) Yea, though I walk through the valley of the shadow of death, I will fear no evil; For You are with me; Your rod and Your staff, they comfort me. (5) You prepare a table before me in the presence of my enemies; You anoint my head with oil; My cup runs over. (6) Surely goodness and mercy shall follow me All the days of my life; And I will dwell in the house of the LORD Forever.*

My Rest-Giver.

Let us look at verse 2 – *"(2) He makes me to lie down in green pastures".*

God makes me lie down – He makes me rest. What can we learn about God, our rest-giver, from this single statement?

1. **God's Rest Is A Required Place For Us.**

   The phrase "He makes me to lie down" (Strong's H7257 = râbats [raw-bats]) is one word in the Hebrew language. It means "to cause to crouch down, or recline, or lay down, or to make rest".

   Often, we get so busy that we avoid taking time to rest. We may think that rest is an enemy of productivity, and that rest keeps us from getting things done that need to be done.

But the Bible says that God wants us to rest – it is His will that we take time to rest.

Matthew 11:28, NIV – *(28) "Come to me, all you who are weary and burdened, and I will give you rest."*

God invites us to come to Him and receive rest from Him. But what if we do not respond to His invitation to enter into His rest?

Psalm 23 verse two says that God **MAKES** us lie down and rest. So if we do not respond to His invitation, and come to Him and receive His rest, He loves us so much, and He so much wants us to receive His rest, that He will MAKE us to lie down and rest.

And if we resist His rest, we are resisting the will and purpose of God.

Could it be that some of our fatigue, is not the fatigue that comes from not resting, but the fatigue that comes from resisting God, as He tries to give us His rest?

When will we realize that whenever we fight with God, whenever we resist God, we **WILL** lose, and we will lose in so many ways? We will lose His strength, we will lose His blessing, we will lose His favour, we will lose His peace, and so much more.

He so much wants us to rest, that if we do not take the time to rest, in His love, He will "make us to rest". He will make us to stop what we are doing and take the time to rest.

It would seem to be a smart thing to take time to rest, rather than be forced by God to rest!

Hebrews 4:11, NIV – *"(11) Let us, therefore, make every effort to enter that rest ..."*

God wants us to remove every hindrance, and every distraction, and take the time to rest, and receive His rest.

2. God's Rest Is A Revitalizing Place For Us.

The word "Green" (Strong's H1877 = דֶּשֶׁא [deshe']) means "tender grass, tender herb, a sprout". And as we know, a sprout is a new growth that springs up.

So, the place of rest that God has prepared for us is a green place – it is a place filled with life. That place is tender, it is soft, it is a place that invites rest.

It is also a place with herb-like properties – for our health and for our refreshing. And it is a place that causes new growth in our lives.

Psalm 91:1, NIV – *(1) He who dwells in the shelter of the Most High <u>will rest in the shadow of the Almighty</u>.*

When we respond to God's invitation to rest, we enter into His shade, His shelter, and receive His refreshing.

I wonder if we would be more willing to take the time to rest, if we understood that God has promised that if we do, He would revitalize us, refresh us, and give us new life?

3. God's Rest Is A Pleasant And Safe Place For Us.

The word "Pasture" (Strong's H4999 = נָאָה [nâ'âh]) means "a pasture, a home, a place of habitation, a pleasant place".

God reveals in Psalm 23 that His place of rest is a pleasant place, a safe place, a place that feels like

"Home". If we allow Him to take us to His place of rest, we will actually enjoy it!

After a while, coming into God's rest will no longer feel foreign to us. Instead, it will feel like our favorite vacation spot, where we can stop, live, and enjoy.

1 John 3:19, NIV – *(19) "... we set our hearts at rest in his presence."*

When we make the choice to set our hearts on God's invitation to rest, it will be a place where we can thoroughly enjoy God's presence.

4. God's Rest Is A Dwelling Place For Us.

Remember that the word "Pasture" (Strong's H4999 = נָאָה [nâ'âh]) means "a pasture, a home, a place of habitation, a pleasant place".

So, Psalm 23:2 also says that God's place of rest for us is to be a place of habitation. That means that we can go there to rest, we can receive rest, and we can take that place of rest with us as we get up. God wants us to enter into that place of rest, stay in that place of rest, and then live and minister from that place of rest.

Hebrews 4:9-11, NIV – *(9) There remains, then, a Sabbath-rest for the people of God; (10) for anyone who enters God's rest also rests from his own work, just as God did from his. (11) Let us, therefore, make every effort to enter that rest ....".*

The Sabbath-rest is more than a day of rest – it is a way of living in the rest of God. And in that place of rest, we rest from OUR work, our striving, and our labouring, and instead, we do God's work, with His strength, His energy, His vitality, while living in our place of rest in Him.

So, if the Lord is our Shepherd, and we allow Him, He will bring us into a dwelling place where everything we do, we will do from a place of rest in Him.

When He says move, we should move, and when He says lay down, we should lay down. And when we stop moving, we are to be in a place of rest, and when we start moving, we can still be in a place of rest.

And we can trust God that our time of inactivity will be just as productive as our time of activity, because we will be living in rest, and the Lord will be our rest-giver.

Prayer.

"Father, help me to not fight You, when You endeavour to make me to lie down. Help me to find that required place of rest that You have for me. Help me to find that revitalizing place of rest that You have for me. Help me to find that pleasant and safe place of rest that You have for me. And help me to find that dwelling place of rest that You have for me. In Jesus' name. Amen!

Reminder: How To Meditate.

1. Study Thoughtfully.
2. Speak To Ourselves.
3. Speak To God.
4. Imagine / Picture.
5. Contemplate and Reflect.

Assignment.

1. For the next number of days, take time every day to mediate on God as your "Rest-Giver".

2. Ask Him to reveal to you different aspects of the fact that:

    - God's place of rest is a required place for us.
    - God's place of rest is a revitalizing place for us.
    - God's place of rest is a pleasant and safe place for us.
    - God's place of rest is a dwelling place for us.

3. Picture yourself entering that place of rest, lying down, becoming revitalized, and then living from the place of rest.

4. Record any insights God gives you and meditate on them.

Part 10 – Knowing God As My Guide

A Crisis Look At Psalm 23.

We are looking at Psalm 23, to help us learn how we can draw closer to God during a time of crisis.

Psalm 23:1-6, NKJV – *(1) The LORD is my shepherd; I shall not want. (2) He makes me to lie down in green pastures; He leads me beside the still waters. (3) He restores my soul; He leads me in the paths of righteousness For His name's sake. (4) Yea, though I walk through the valley of the shadow of death, I will fear no evil; For You are with me; Your rod and Your staff, they comfort me. (5) You prepare a table before me in the presence of my enemies; You anoint my head with oil; My cup runs over. (6) Surely goodness and mercy shall follow me All the days of my life; And I will dwell in the house of the LORD Forever.*

My Guide.

Let us look at verse 2 – *"(2)* ***He leads me*** *beside the still waters".*

The phrase "He leads me (Strong's H5095 = נָהַל [nâhal]) means "to run with a sparkle or to flow, to conduct and protect, to sustain, to carry, to lead and guide gently."

So how does God guide me?

1. God Guides Us To Refresh Us.

The first meaning of the word "lead" is "to run with a sparkle or to flow". We all know that the cleanest and purist water is in a flowing river.

So, when God guides us, our lives will never become stagnant or stale. Instead, God guides us as a flowing river, and as He guides us, He refreshes us, and revitalizes us.

Jeremiah 31:25, NIV – *(25) "I will refresh the weary and satisfy the faint."*

So as God guides us, He refreshes us.

2. God Guides Us To Protect Us.

The second mean of the word "lead" is "to conduct and protect".

So, we never have to worry about our safety when we are being led by God. As God guides us, He conducts or orders our lives, and He protects us from danger and harm.

Proverbs 2:8, NIV – *(8) for he guards the course of the just and protects the way of his faithful ones.*

3. God Guides Us To Strengthen Us.

The third meaning of the word "lead" is "to sustain", which means, "to strengthen".

So as God guides us, He sustains us – He gives us fresh strength and energy. As God guides us, He strengthens us, so that we can do whatever He has called us to do.

Isaiah 40:29, NIV – *(29) He gives strength to the weary and increases the power of the weak.*

4. God Guides Us To Keep Me.

The fourth meaning of the word "lead" is "to carry".

As God guides us, there will be times that will be difficult, and if left to our own ability, we may come to ruin.

However, throughout our lives, when the way gets too tough, God will actually carry us, so that He can keep us in His care and love.

Psalm 28:9, NIV – *(9) Save your people and bless your inheritance; be their shepherd and carry them forever.*

5. God Guides Us With Gentleness.

The fifth meaning of the word "lead" is "to lead and guide gently."

When God guides us, He does so with gentleness. We never have to fear that He will shove us into something. He will guide us in a way that we are able to follow without fear.

Matthew 11:29, NIV – *(29) Take my yoke upon you and learn from me, for I am gentle and humble in heart, and you will find rest for your souls.*

6. God Guides Us With His Peace.

Psalm 23:2, NIV - *(2) He leads me beside the still waters".*

Now, the first thing we need to notice, is that this verse doesn't say that God leads us TO still waters, He doesn't take us to a nice, quiet lake, where we can set up a tent, and just sit there.

No, it says "he leads me BESIDE the still waters", meaning that throughout the whole course of our lives, we can walk along a river of still water.

Remember Psalm 1:3, NIV – *"He is like a tree planted by streams of water ...".*

So even though the righteous can be like a tree planted by streams of water, the water can actually move with us, throughout our lives, so that during our whole life, we can continuously draw from this God-birthed still water.

Now, let us look even deeper ...

The word "beside" (Strong's H5921 = עַל ['al]) means "to be above, over, upon, or against with a downward aspect".

So as God guides us beside the still waters, our actual vantage point is that we are walking <u>OVER</u> or <u>ON</u> the still waters, wherever we walk.

The word "still" (Strong's H4496 = מְנוּחָה [menûchâh]) means "repose, peaceful, consoling, comfortable, quiet, restful, still".

So, Psalm 23 tells us that God guides us to walk above or on peaceful waters. That means, that as He guides us, peace will be our foundation, and our companion.

Luke 1:79, NIV – *(79) … to guide our feet <u>into the path of peace</u>.*

Isaiah 55:12, NIV – *(12) You will go out in joy and <u>be led forth in peace</u> …*

So as God guides us, we will not be anxious or fearful. Instead, God will guide us with a constant foundation and companion of peace.

Philippians 4:7, NIV – *(7) And <u>the peace of God</u>, which transcends all understanding, <u>will guard your hearts and your minds in Christ Jesus</u>.*

7. God Guides Us Into Life.

The word "waters" (Strong's H4325 = מַיִם [mayim]) means "water, juice, life-giving fluid".

So those waters of peace that we are to walk on, are also waters of life. They are refreshing waters, waters that give energy, waters filled with life.

So as God guides us, He guides us into life. He refreshes us, He invigorates us, He energies us. We will never become overwhelmed or exhausted if we let God guide us, because He reenergizes us as He leads us.

John 14:6, NIV – *(6) Jesus answered, "I am the way and the truth and the life. ..."*

Prayer.

"Father, help me to allow You to guide me. You guide me to refresh me, so that I will never be stagnant in my life. You guide me to protect me, so I will always be safe as You guide me. You guide me to strengthen me, so I will always have the energy I need. You guide me to keep me, so I will never fall away from You. You guide me with gentleness, so I will never feel forced by You. You guide me with peace, so I will always be at rest in You. And You give me into life, and so I will stay refreshed in You".

"Thank You that I can always trust You as my guide. In Jesus' name. Amen!

Reminder: How To Meditate.

1. Study Thoughtfully.
2. Speak To Ourselves.
3. Speak To God.
4. Imagine / Picture.

5. Contemplate and Reflect.

Assignment.

1. For the next number of days, take time every day to mediate on God as your "Guide".

2. Ask Him to reveal to you different aspects of the fact that:

   - God guides us to refresh us.
   - God guides us to protect us.
   - God guides us to strengthen us.
   - God guides us to keep us.
   - God guides us with gentleness.
   - God guides us with peace.
   - God guides us into life.

3. Picture yourself being guided by God and experiencing each aspect of His guidance.

4. Record any insights God gives you and meditate on them.

Part 11 – Knowing God As My Restorer

A Crisis Look At Psalm 23.

We are looking at Psalm 23, to help us learn how we can draw closer to God during a time of crisis.

Psalm 23:1-6, NKJV – *(1) The LORD is my shepherd; I shall not want. (2) He makes me to lie down in green pastures; He leads me beside the still waters. (3) He restores my soul; He leads me in the paths of righteousness For His name's sake. (4) Yea, though I walk through the valley of the shadow of death, I will fear no evil; For You are with me; Your rod and Your staff, they comfort me. (5) You prepare a table before me in the presence of my enemies; You anoint my head with oil; My cup runs over. (6) Surely goodness and mercy shall follow me All the days of my life; And I will dwell in the house of the LORD Forever.*

My Restorer.

Let us look at verse 3 – *"(3) He restores my soul".*

The word "restores" (Strong's H7725 = שׁוּב [shûb]) means "to turn back, to retreat, to deliver, to refresh".

The word "soul" (Strong's H5315 = נֶפֶשׁ [nephesh]) means "a breathing creature, vitality, person". So, we are talking about the whole person – spirit, soul, and body.

So how is God our restorer – spirit, soul, and body?

1. **He Restores Us To Our Previous Condition.**

   The first meaning of the word "restore" is "to turn back", meaning, "to restore to a previous condition".

So, if we have hope, and we lose our hope, God restores us by giving us fresh hope. If we have joy and we lose our joy, God restores us by giving us fresh joy. If we have peace and we lose our peace, God restores us by giving us fresh peace. If we have passion and we lose our passion, God restores us by giving us fresh passion.

No matter what God has given us, if, for any reason, we lose some of it, due to the disappointments or challenges of life, God wants to restore it, to give it back to us.

Jeremiah 30:17, NIV – *(17) "… I will restore you to health and heal your wounds," declares the LORD,*

2. **He Restores Us To A Place Of Safety.**

The second meaning of the word "restore" is "to retreat". Now, it does not mean "retreat" in the sense of running away because we are being defeated. Instead, it means "retreat" in the sense of going to a place of safety, where we can rest, renew our strength, re-strategize, and begin to move forward again.

When we go off to a quiet place to renew ourselves, we say that we are going on a "retreat". We are not being defeated or surrendering – we are getting alone to renew and re-energize and re-strategize.

There are times in our lives when we will feel overwhelmed, where we really will not be sure what to do, and we will feel totally surrounded by challenges or obstacles.

In those times, God wants to restore us, by moving us into a place of safety, where we can be renewed, and be able to develop a fresh vision and strategy for going forward.

Psalm 32:7, NIV – *(7) "You are my hiding place; you will protect me from trouble ..."*

God restores us by moving us into a place of safety, a hiding place, where He protects us from the onslaught of attack, as He reenergizes us.

Psalm 32:10, NIV – *(10) Many are the woes of the wicked, but the LORD's unfailing love surrounds the man who trusts in him.*

God restores us by taking us to a place of safety, and surrounding us with His love, so that we can be strengthened by Him.

3. He Restores Us To Freedom.

The third meaning of the word "restore" is "to deliver". The word "deliver" means to "set free" – body, soul, and spirit.

Jesus came to set us free!

Isaiah 61:1, NIV – *(1) "The Spirit of the Sovereign LORD is on me, because the LORD has anointed me to preach good news to the poor. He has sent me to bind up the brokenhearted, to proclaim freedom for the captives and release from darkness for the prisoners ..."*

Jesus paid for our freedom when He died on the cross and rose again from the dead. And Jesus, through the Holy Spirit, now ministers or administrates ongoing freedom in our lives.

Romans 8:2, NIV – *(2) because through Christ Jesus the law of the Spirit of life set me free from the law of sin and death.*

So as the Spirit of Christ ministers to us, He sets us increasing free from the law of sin and death, meaning every curse.

Psalm 32:7, NIV – *(7) You ... surround me with songs of deliverance.*

As the Spirit of God sets us increasingly free, He actually surrounds us with songs of deliverance – songs of freedom. Have you ever cooperated with the Spirit of God, and joined with Him in singing a song of deliverance over your life?

4. He Restores Us To Full Life.

The fourth meaning of the word "restore" is "to refresh".

To refresh means to quicken, to enliven, to give life, to revitalize.

As we walk in relationship with God our restorer, He is constantly wanting to reenergize us. He wants to keep filling us afresh with His Holy Spirit, so that we always minister from His strength and life, and not our own.

Ephesians 5:18, NIV – *(18) Do not get drunk on wine, which leads to debauchery. Instead, be filled with the Spirit.*

God wants us to be filled with His life on an ongoing basis.

Ephesians 3:19, NIV – *(19) "and to know this love that surpasses knowledge — that you may be filled to the measure of all the fullness of God."*

The Bible says that the consequence of experiencing God's love is not just so we can feel loved or feel better about ourselves. God's primary purpose for manifesting

His love to us is that we would want to be filled to the full measure of the fulness of God, and want to live by the His life.

Prayer.

"Father, help me to allow You to restore me, each and every day. Restore me to my previous condition of love, joy, peace, patience, kindness, goodness, faithfulness, gentleness, and self-control, as well as my hope and passion for You. Restore me by keeping me safe in You as my hiding place. Restore me by giving me freedom in every area of my life. And restore me by helping me to receive the fulness of Your life, on a daily basis."

"In Jesus' name. Amen!"

Reminder: How To Meditate.

1. Study Thoughtfully.
2. Speak To Ourselves.
3. Speak To God.
4. Imagine / Picture.
5. Contemplate and Reflect.

Assignment.

1. For the next number of days, take time every day to mediate on God as your "Restorer".

2. Ask Him to reveal to you different aspects of the fact that:

    - He restores us to our previous condition.
    - He restores us to a place of safety.
    - He restores us to freedom.
    - He restores us to full life.

3. Picture yourself restored by God and experiencing each aspect of His restoration.

4. Record any insights God gives you and meditate on them.

Part 12 – Knowing God As My Protector

A Crisis Look At Psalm 23.

We are looking at Psalm 23, to help us learn how we can draw closer to God during a time of crisis.

Psalm 23:1-6, NKJV – *(1) The LORD is my shepherd; I shall not want. (2) He makes me to lie down in green pastures; He leads me beside the still waters. (3) He restores my soul; He leads me in the paths of righteousness For His name's sake. (4) Yea, though I walk through the valley of the shadow of death, I will fear no evil; For You are with me; Your rod and Your staff, they comfort me. (5) You prepare a table before me in the presence of my enemies; You anoint my head with oil; My cup runs over. (6) Surely goodness and mercy shall follow me All the days of my life; And I will dwell in the house of the LORD Forever.*

My Protector.

Let us look at verse 3.

Psalm 23:3, NIV – *(3) "He leads me in the paths of righteousness for His name's sake."*

1. **God Has Paths Of Protection For Us.**

   The word "paths" (Strong's H4570 = מַעְגָּל [ma'gâl]) means "a round track, a circular rampart, a protective trench".

   A **trench**, as we know, is a long path in the ground, where a person can go for protection. During a conflict, soldiers would dig a deep trench, and they would fight from the protection of the trench, and be protected from the bullets or arrows of the enemy, yet still be able to look up out of the trench and see what the enemy was doing.

A **rampart** is the same idea as a trench, but is like an elevated trench on top of a wall, so that the solders could walk along the elevated path, and be protected from the enemy because of the walls on the sides of the rampart, and be able to look down to the ground below to see what the enemy was doing.

And this Hebrew word also indicates that it is circular, so we are protected from the enemy in every direction.

So, Psalm 23 verse 3 it is not just talking about a foot path, but a path with protective walls on all sides, almost like a fortress of protection.

2. God's Paths Of Protection Are Righteousness.

Psalm 23:3 – *(3) "He leads me in the paths of righteousness for His name's sake."*

So, God has very specific paths for us – paths of protection. And what are those paths of protection? God gives us paths or trenches or ramparts of **righteousness** on all sides to protect us.

The word "righteousness" (Strong's H6664 = צֶדֶק [tsedeq]) means "righteousness", including "moral and legal righteousness".

So the Lord wants to lead us into paths of protection, and those paths of protection are moral righteousness (which causes us to live righteous lives), and legal righteousness (which causes us to be declared to be legally righteous or "not guilty" by a judge).

Proverbs 11:6, NIV – *"The righteousness of the upright delivers them ..."*

The paths or trenches or ramparts of righteousness protect us, because living righteous and being legally righteous is what delivers us from our enemies.

Proverbs 12:28, NkJV – *"In the way of righteousness there is life, and in its pathway there is no death."*

The paths or trenches or ramparts of righteousness protect us, and give us life, because the paths of righteousness are the paths of life.

Isaiah 32:17, NIV – *(17) The fruit of righteousness will be peace; the effect of righteousness will be quietness and confidence forever.*

Righteousness has fruit, and that fruit is peace – peace with God and peace with other people, including peace with our enemies. And righteousness has an effect – internal quietness and confidence forever.

So, a life of righteousness will protect us from turmoil, and strife, and so much more.

3. God Places Us Into His Righteousness

Psalm 23:3 – *(3) "He leads me in the paths of righteousness for His name's sake."*

The phrase "He leads me" used in this verse 3, is a different Hebrew word than the one used in verse 2.

Here, the phrase "He leads me" (Strong's H5148 = נָחָה [nâchâh]) means "to transport or bring or put to a new location", or "to govern or to straighten".

The first meaning of the word "leads" is "to transport or bring or put to a new location".

Because of Jesus's death on the cross for our sins, God **transported** us into **His** righteousness. We were NOT righteous, but through the death of Christ, God transported us into His righteousness. He gives or imputes righteousness to us.

Romans 3:22, NIV – *(22) This righteousness from God comes through faith in Jesus Christ to all who believe.*

Romans 5:17, NIV – *(17) "... those who receive God's abundant provision of grace and of the gift of righteousness ..."*

God leads us, He transports us, He brings us, He puts us into a completely new place – the place of righteousness – because of the sacrificial death of Jesus on the cross, and we are now declared legally righteous or "not guilty" by our judge – God Himself.

4. God Governs Us With His Righteousness.

The second meaning of the word "leads" is "to govern". God GOVERNS us with His righteousness.

2 Timothy 2:22, NIV – *"Flee the evil desires of youth, and pursue righteousness ...".*

As we pursue and experience the righteousness that God has given us, that righteousness governs our lives, and turns us from the wrong desires of youthfulness, and causes us to become morally righteous.

Philippians 1:11, NIV – *(11) "filled with the fruit of righteousness that comes through Jesus Christ ..."*

As God governs us with His righteousness, He produces much **GOOD** fruit in our lives, so that we become manifest moral righteousness.

5. God Straightens Us With His Righteousness.

The third meaning of the word "leads" is "to straighten". One of the ways that God governs us, is by straightening out the crooked things in our lives with His righteousness.

Psalm 27:11, NIV – *(11) Teach me your way, O LORD; lead me in a straight path.*

And that word "lead" there means "to transport, to govern, to straighten". So as God leads us into His righteousness, He makes our paths straight.

Proverbs 4:11, NIV – *(11) I guide you in the way of wisdom and lead you along straight paths.*

God's righteousness is the way of wisdom, and as He leads us into His righteousness, He straightens out every crooked issue, every distorted thought, and every wayward behaviour in our lives.

So, God gives us His righteousness, through Christ. He transports us into His righteousness and makes us legally righteous. And He governs us with His righteousness, and straightens us with His righteousness, so that we can be morally righteous.

6. Manifesting God's Righteousness Honors God.

Psalm 23:3 – *(3) "He leads me in the paths of righteousness for His name's sake."*

The phrase "for his name's sake" means "for the purpose of giving honour to him".

So if we allow God to be our protector, by transporting or placing us into His righteousness, our lives will be protected by His righteousness in us, and our lives will be transformed by His righteousness working in us, so that our lives will always bring glory to Him.

Prayer.

"Father, help me to allow You to be my protector. Father, by faith, I fully receive Your gift of righteousness in my life, paid by the sacrificial death of Your Son, Jesus, on the cross. Thank You for giving me the righteousness that I could never attain in myself."

"I now choose to allow You to govern my life by Your righteousness, and straighten out every crooked way in my life, so that I may glorify You in everything that I do."

"In Jesus' name. Amen!"

Reminder: How To Meditate.

1. Study Thoughtfully.
2. Speak To Ourselves.
3. Speak To God.
4. Imagine / Picture.
5. Contemplate and Reflect.

Assignment.

1. For the next number of days, take time every day to mediate on God as your "Protector".

2. Ask Him to reveal to you different aspects of the fact that:

    - God has paths of protection for us.
    - God's paths of protection are righteousness.
    - God places us into His righteousness
    - God governs us with His righteousness.
    - God straightens us with His righteousness.

- As we manifest God's righteousness in our lives, it honors God.

3. Picture yourself being protected by God, as His puts you into the centre of His righteousness, and governs and straightens every aspect of your life by His righteousness.

4. Picture every aspect of your life glorifying God.

5. Record any insights God gives you and meditate on them.

Part 13 – Knowing God As My Courage-Giver

A Crisis Look At Psalm 23.

We are looking at Psalm 23, to help us learn how we can draw closer to God during a time of crisis.

Psalm 23:1-6, NKJV – *(1) The LORD is my shepherd; I shall not want. (2) He makes me to lie down in green pastures; He leads me beside the still waters. (3) He restores my soul; He leads me in the paths of righteousness For His name's sake. (4) Yea, though I walk through the valley of the shadow of death, I will fear no evil; For You are with me; Your rod and Your staff, they comfort me. (5) You prepare a table before me in the presence of my enemies; You anoint my head with oil; My cup runs over. (6) Surely goodness and mercy shall follow me All the days of my life; And I will dwell in the house of the LORD Forever.*

My Courage-Giver.

Let us look at verse 4.

Psalm 23:4, NIV – *(4) Yea, though I walk through the valley of the shadow of death, I will fear no evil; for You are with me."*

1. **We Can Stand Strong In The Face Of Death.**

   Psalm 23:4, NIV – *(4) Yea, though I walk through <u>the valley of the shadow of death</u>, I will fear no evil; for You are with me;"*

   The word "valley" (Strong's H1516 = gah'ee [gay']) means "a narrow gorge with high and lofty sides, a deep valley with shear sides".

So, the "valley" is actually more like a canyon or a chasm, than a valley.

The phrase "shadow of death" (Strong's H6757 = צַלְמָוֶת [tsalmâveth]) means "shadow or shade of death (the grave)".

So when we draw close to God, even when we feel completely hemmed in by the circumstances, even when we are concerned that the situation might result in harm, or even loss of our life, even when we are completely unsure of what the outcome will be, we can still stand strong in the face of every challenge.

Hebrews 2:14-15, NIV – *(14) ... by his [Jesus'] death he might destroy him who holds the power of death — that is, the devil — (15) and free those who all their lives were held in slavery by their fear of death.*

Jesus has already dealt with the enemy of death, and in Christ, we can be eternally secure, no matter how bleak the situation, because God is with us.

2. We Can Live Without Fear.

Psalm 23:4, NIV – *(4) Yea, though I walk through the valley of the shadow of death, I will fear no evil; for You are with me."*

The word "fear" (Strong's H3372 = יָרֵא [yârê']) means "to be afraid of or to dread", "to revere, to be in reverence of".

The word "evil" (Strong's H7451 = רַע [ra']) means "bad, natural or moral evil, adversity, affliction, calamity, wickedness".

The first meaning of the word "fear" is "to be afraid of or to dread".

So, when we draw close to God, we do not have to live with fear of the consequences of the crisis we are in. We do not have to fear that affliction or calamity or adversity will come upon us. We do not have to obsess or even entertain thoughts about all the bad things that may happen. We do not have to fear, or worry, or be anxious. We can live without fear.

Psalm 91:5-6, NIV – *(5) You will not fear the terror of night, nor the arrow that flies by day, (6) nor the pestilence that stalks in the darkness, nor the plague that destroys at midday.*

No matter whether the situation is war, or pestilence or plague, or even something completely unknown, we do not need to fear, because God is with us.

3. We Can Live Without Compromise.

Psalm 23:4, NIV – *(4) Yea, though I walk through the valley of the shadow of death, I will fear no evil; for You are with me."*

The second meaning of the word "fear" is "to revere or be in reverence of". It means to "feel a deep respect or admiration" for something.

Psalm 23 says that when we draw close to God in a time of crisis, we do not have to admire evil, or look at doing evil as an option to escape our problems.

If we are concerned over our finances, we do not have to lie about them, in order to protect our money. If we are concerned about our health, we do not have to make up a story in order to get medical treatment. If we are concerned about the consequences of our actions, we do not have to distort the truth to escape punishment.

We do not have to ever consider evil as an option in order to protect ourselves.

1 Peter 2:16, NIV – *(16) Live as free men, but do not use your freedom as a cover-up for evil; live as servants of God.*

When we draw close to God, we will not "revere" evil – we will not consider evil as an option in order to protect ourselves. We do not need to compromise our integrity, in order to reduce the possibility of bad consequences. Instead, we can live without compromise because God is with us.

4. **We Can Live With Confidence In God's Presence.**

Psalm 23:4, NIV – *(4) Yea, though I walk through the valley of the shadow of death, I will fear no evil; for You are with me;"*

The word "for" (Strong's H3588 = כִּי [kîy]) means "surely, certainly, truly".

So why can we live without being afraid? Why can we live without compromise? Because we can be completely certain, beyond a shadow of a doubt, that God is with us.

You see, as we draw close to God in a time of crisis, we will become acutely aware of His presence with us, and when we are acutely aware of the presence of our loving heavenly Father, His perfect love drives all fear out of our lives.

1 John 4:18, NIV – *(18) There is no fear in love. But perfect love drives out fear …*

5. We Can Know That God Is Always With Us.

Psalm 23:4, NIV – *(4) Yea, though I walk through the valley of the shadow of death, I will fear no evil; for You are with me."*

The word "with me" (Strong's H5978 = עִמָּד [ʽimmâd]) means "along with, accompanying, mine that I have received".

God is not just "with us" – meaning that He is on our side, that He is for us. Instead, God is "with us" – meaning that He is accompanying us, every step of our live, and every second of our day. He is so much with us in every moment, that not only we are His, but He is ours!

Song of Solomon 6:3, NIV – *"I am my beloved's, and my beloved is mine: ..."*

God, the lover of our soul, is always with us. We belong to Him, and He belongs to us. We have given our lives in covenant with Him, and He has given His life in covenant with us.

So, we can always have the courage to face whatever comes against us.

Prayer.

"Father, help me to allow You to be my courage-giver. Father, by faith, I accept the fact that You are always with me, in every situation, every second of the day. And because You are with me, I do not need to fear any circumstance, I do not need to compromise my integrity, for You will help me when I need it. And I do not need to fear even death, because my life is eternally secure in you."

"Thank You, Lord. In Jesus' name. Amen!"

Reminder: How To Meditate.

1. Study Thoughtfully.
2. Speak To Ourselves.
3. Speak To God.
4. Imagine / Picture.
5. Contemplate and Reflect.

Assignment.

1. For the next number of days, take time every day to mediate on God as your "Courage-Giver".

2. Ask Him to reveal to you different aspects of the fact that:

    - We can stand strong in the face of death.
    - We can live without fear.
    - We can live without compromise.
    - We can live with confidence in God's presence.
    - We can know that God is always with us.

3. Picture yourself standing strong in courage, no matter what comes against you. See yourself living without fear or compromise, as you walk side-by-side with God every day, and in every circumstance.

4. Record any insights God gives you and meditate on them.

Part 14 – Knowing God As My Comforter

A Crisis Look At Psalm 23.

We are looking at Psalm 23, to help us learn how we can draw closer to God during a time of crisis.

Psalm 23:1-6, NKJV – *(1) The LORD is my shepherd; I shall not want. (2) He makes me to lie down in green pastures; He leads me beside the still waters. (3) He restores my soul; He leads me in the paths of righteousness For His name's sake. (4) Yea, though I walk through the valley of the shadow of death, I will fear no evil; For You are with me; Your rod and Your staff, they comfort me. (5) You prepare a table before me in the presence of my enemies; You anoint my head with oil; My cup runs over. (6) Surely goodness and mercy shall follow me All the days of my life; And I will dwell in the house of the LORD Forever.*

My Comforter

Let us look at verse 4 – *(4) "... Your rod and Your staff, they comfort me."*

1. We Can Live Without Anxiety.

The word "comfort" (Strong's H5162 = נָחַם [nâcham]) means "to breathe a sigh of relief, to be consoled or comforted, to be put at ease".

Have you ever received news from someone, that something bad might happen? Perhaps you were told that you may be audited, and suddenly you experienced some anxiety, because you knew that it could result in a lot of work. Perhaps you were told that a loved one was on a trip, and no one had heard from them in days, and suddenly you experienced some inner dread. Perhaps you were told that your company was downsizing, and there were going to be several layoffs, and suddenly you felt fear.

But then you discovered that you were not going to be audited after all. Or you heard that your loved one had contacted a family member and they were fine. Or your boss told you not to worry, because your job was secure.

And what happened? We breathed a sigh of relief, we were consoled or comforted by the good news, and our heart and emotions were put at ease.

The Bible tells us that this is how we can live when God is our Shepherd, even in a time of crisis. We can live with a heart at ease, a heart without anxiety, a heart comforted or consoled by the presence of God in our lives.

How is that possible? Two reasons … God's rod and God's staff.

GOD'S ROD.

Psalm 32:4, NIV – *(4) "... Your rod and Your staff, they comfort me."*

The word "rod" (Strong's H7626 = שֵׁבֶט [shêbeṭ]) means "a stick, a rod, a staff or a sceptre for punishing, fighting and ruling".

The purpose of the rod is three-fold: to **punish**, to **fight or do battle**, and **to rule**.

2. **We Are Comforted By God's Rod Of Punishment.**

We can be comforted by God's rod of punishment.

We can know, beyond a shadow of a doubt, that God will deal with those who try to hurt us. We do not ever have to try to "get even" with those who come against us. God has promised that He will punish all those who come against us.

Romans 12:19, NIV – *(19) Do not take revenge, my friends, but leave room for God's wrath, for it is written: "It is mine to avenge; I will repay," says the Lord.*

Because God is completely just, only He has the right to punish. And because God is completely omniscient – He is all-knowing, only God has the ability to punish appropriately – not too lenient, and not too harsh.

So, we can be comforted, knowing that God will administer a just and righteous punishment for our enemies.

3. We Are Comforted By God's Rod Of Warfare.

We are also comforted by God's rod of warfare – for He does battle on our behalf.

When someone comes against us, we can try to fight back, we can get involved in a messy battle of trying to get the upper hand, OR … we can just let God fight on our behalf.

Deuteronomy 20:4, NIV – *(4) "For the LORD your God is the one who goes with you to fight for you against your enemies to give you victory."*

So, whenever someone comes against us, they are coming against our God, and so we are comforted by the fact that, since God is with us, He will fight our battles for us.

4. We Am Comforted By God's Rod Of Rule.

We are also comforted by God's rod of rule – for He rules over every situation. When anything comes against us, we are comforted that God is ruler. He has all power, and all authority, and He will ensure that His will is done in every situation.

Psalm 22:28- NIV – *(28) for dominion belongs to the LORD and he rules over the nations.*

Psalm 66:7, NIV – *(7) He rules forever by his power, his eyes watch the nations — let not the rebellious rise up against him. Selah*

God is on the throne, He rules over heaven and earth, and He rules over every situation. And so, we can be comforted, that because God rules, He rules over the circumstances of our lives, and He only allows those things that are according to His divine purposes for us.

GOD'S STAFF.

The word "staff" (Strong's H4938 = מִשְׁעֵנָה [mish'ênâh]) means "a support or a walking stick".

A shepherd's staff had three primary functions.

First, the staff functioned as a **walking stick**, to keep the shepherd stable while walking on rocky ground. Second, the staff functioned as a **rescue stick**, as the curved handle was wide enough to fit around a sheep or goat that had fallen down into a crevice. And third, the staff functioned as a **guiding stick**, to correct or redirect the sheep or goats back onto the right path.

5. **We Are Comforted By God's Staff Of Stability.**

So first, we are comforted by God's staff of stability.

As we walk through the difficult seasons of our life, God reaches out to us with His staff, to give us stability, so that we do not stumble and fall because of the challenges of life.

Proverbs 3:23, NIV – *(23) Then you will go on your way in safety, and <u>your foot will not stumble</u>.*

Yes, we may face many challenges in life, and some of them may be quite difficult. But as we draw close to God in a time of crisis, He has promised to use His staff of stability, so that we will NOT stumble no matter where our feet take me.

6. We Are Comforted By God's Staff Of Deliverance.

We are also comforted by God's staff of deliverance, His rescue stick.

Sometimes things come against us, and we do not even have time to react, and we suddenly find ourselves falling into a pit, and being ensnared in a trap of the enemy.

Thank God, that in moments like that, God takes His staff of rescue – His staff of deliverance, and He extends it gently toward us, and pulls us out of the pit that has tried to trap us.

Psalm 40:2, NIV – *(2) <u>He lifted me out of the slimy pit</u>, out of the mud and mire; he set my feet on a rock and gave me a firm place to stand.*

Thank God that whether we innocently fall into a pit, or we do so because of some foolish decision in our own life, God our shepherd will reach down and deliver us out of that pit, and set our feet back on a secure and firm place to stand.

7. We Are Comforted By God's Staff Of Correction.

We are also comforted by God's staff of correction.

You see, I do not know about you, but I know myself all too well. I know I am not always led by God's Spirit and God's Word. I know I sometimes wander in the wrong direction by mistake, or even foolishly make a choice to investigate something that I know probably will not be good for me. Either way, I may find myself walking off of God's path for my life, and straying down a path that can lead to danger.

Thank God for His staff of correction!

Proverbs 15:32, NIV – *(32) He who ignores discipline despises himself, but <u>whoever heeds correction gains understanding</u>.*

Revelation 3:19, NIV – *(19) <u>Those whom I love I rebuke and discipline</u>. So be earnest, and repent.*

Thank God that no matter how foolish we are, or how foolish our decisions are, we are comforted by the fact that God our Shepherd is just waiting to guide us back onto the right path, by His staff of correction.

Prayer.

"Father, help me to allow You to be my comforter."

"Thank You, God, that I can live without any anxiety in my heart. Thank you that You will use your ROD, to punish my enemies, do battle on my behalf, and rule over every situation that I may face. Thank You that You will also use your STAFF, to give me stability during the challenging times of life, deliver me from all danger, and bring me correction to get back on the right path whenever I stray."

"What an incredible and loving God You are! Thank You for the comfort I am receiving even right now, since You are my Shepherd. And I can draw close to You, in any time of crisis."

Reminder: How To Meditate.

1. Study Thoughtfully.
2. Speak To Ourselves.
3. Speak To God.
4. Imagine / Picture.
5. Contemplate and Reflect.

Assignment.

1. For the next number of days, take time every day to mediate on God as your "Comforter".

2. Ask Him to reveal to you different aspects of the fact that:

    - We can live without anxiety.
    - We are comforted by God's rod of punishment.
    - We are comforted by God's rod of warfare.
    - We are comforted by God's rod of rule.
    - We are comforted by God's staff of stability.
    - We are comforted by God's staff of deliverance.
    - We are comforted by God's staff of correction.

3. Picture God standing beside your Shepherd and see Him holding His rod and staff. See him coming against all of your enemies with His rod of punishment, His rod of warfare and His rod of rule. See him help you with His staff of stability, His staff of deliverance, and His staff of correction. And see all anxiety leaving your heart, as you receive His comfort.

4. Record any insights God gives you and meditate on them.

Part 15 – Knowing God As My Vindicator

A Crisis Look At Psalm 23.

We are looking at Psalm 23, to help us learn how we can draw closer to God during a time of crisis.

Psalm 23:1-6, NKJV – *(1) The LORD is my shepherd; I shall not want. (2) He makes me to lie down in green pastures; He leads me beside the still waters. (3) He restores my soul; He leads me in the paths of righteousness For His name's sake. (4) Yea, though I walk through the valley of the shadow of death, I will fear no evil; For You are with me; Your rod and Your staff, they comfort me. (5) You prepare a table before me in the presence of my enemies; You anoint my head with oil; My cup runs over. (6) Surely goodness and mercy shall follow me All the days of my life; And I will dwell in the house of the LORD Forever.*

My Vindicator

Psalm 23:5, NIV – *(5) You **prepare** a **table** before me in the presence of my enemies.*

1. **God Vindicates Us By Blessing Us With Provision.**

   The word "prepare" (Strong's H6186 = עָרַךְ ['ârak]) means "to set in a row, to put in order, to arrange, to prepare".

   The word "table" (Strong's H7979 = שֻׁלְחָן [shûlchân]) means "a spread-out table, a meal, a feast".

   Our Shepherd God wants to prepare and set out a table in front of us. This table is not for others, it is just for us, it is set out in front of us.

   This table is also a spread-out table. It is not an empty table, a sparse table, or a meager table – it is a spread-out table. It is a table filled with lots of good things for us, and we are free to enjoy all of it. It is a feast.

Psalm 66:12, NIV – *(12) … we went through fire and water, but you brought us to <u>a place of abundance</u>.*

In the middle of a crisis, and especially when things try to come against us, God will vindicate us by providing for us everything we need.

2. God Vindicates Us By Humbling Our Enemies.

Psalm 23:5, NIV – *(5) You prepare a table before me in the <u>presence</u> of my <u>enemies</u>.*

The word "presence" (Strong's H5048 = נֶגֶד [neged]) means "in front of, in the sight of, a place where people can view".

The word "enemies" (Strong's H687 = צָרַר [tsârar]) means "to cramp, to afflict, to besiege, to bind, to cause distress, to oppress, to cause trouble".

So, when we face adversity or crisis, God provides for us and displays our blessing in front of those who are against us.

God sets the table in front of our enemies, and we are allowed to enjoy it without fear of danger. We do not have to grab something and then run away and hide. We are free to actually sit down, even in front of our enemies, and enjoy what God has provided for us.

Our enemies may be literal people that have come against us, or our enemies may be situations or circumstances that try to bind us, oppress us, and cause us distress. However, we are free to sit in front of them, and face them, and not be bound by them.

And there is NOTHING our enemies can do, to keep us from enjoying the table of God. In fact, those who tried to oppress us must sit and stare at our blessing, while we enjoy the provision of God.

Isaiah 54:17, NIV – *(17) No weapon forged against you will prevail, and you will refute every tongue that accuses you. This is the heritage of the servants of the LORD, and this is their vindication from me," declares the LORD.*

In our time of crisis, God wants to put a table of provision before us, even in the presence of those who would try to hinder us, trouble us, or hurt us. Even though we may have people coming against us, God wants to vindicate us by blessing us in front of them. And the blessing we receive from God, vindicates us in front of our enemies.

3. **God Vindicates Us By Preparing The Blessing In Advance.**

Psalm 23:5, NIV – *(5) You prepare a table before me in the presence of my enemies.*

As I said, the word "prepare" (Strong's H6186 = עָרַךְ ['ârak]) means "to set in a row, to arrange, to put in order, to prepare".

God knows what is going to happen to us. In fact, He knows every situation and circumstance that we will ever experience. He knows what will come against us, and what we will be tempted to do when those situations occur. So, God, in His great love and wisdom, prepares for us, in advance, everything we need to overcome every crisis.

Unfortunately, when a crisis comes, our natural response is to try to fix it ourselves. We usually try to overcome the challenge in our own strength and wisdom. We try to fight against our enemies with our own arguments and self-justifications.

But as we try to fight our enemies with our own wisdom and strength, we make some mistakes, and say some foolish things, and do some foolish things.

And then, after wasting our time with a period of self-effort and self-vindication, we come to our senses and turn to God, and we discover that He has already prepared our table of provision for us.

But unfortunately, because of our foolish words and actions, we lessen or tarnish the vindication that God wants to give us.

What God wants us to understand, is that the solution, the provision, the blessing for us was prepared long before we ever faced the crisis. However, we do not experience the solution until we put our eyes on our Shepherd, rather than on the crisis, and embrace His provision. And the sooner we put our eyes on Him, the sooner we will experience His provision.

1 Corinthians 2:9, NIV – *(9) … "No eye has seen, no ear has heard, no mind has conceived what God <u>has prepared</u> for those who love him".*

In the midst of a crisis, we often say, “Where is God in this crisis”? But God is saying “I’m right here with your provision, but you can’t see it because your eyes are still on the crisis, and not on Me”. And the sooner we get our eyes off of the crisis, and the sooner we get our eyes on God, the sooner we will experience the provision and the vindication that God has prepared for us, long ago.

Prayer.

"Father, help me to allow You to be my vindicator."

"Help me to know that You have prepared a blessing of provision for me. Help me to know that I do not have to fight against the crisis, I can simply trust You to fight the battle for me, and humble all of my enemies. And help me to know that the sooner I get my eyes on You, the sooner I will experience Your provision and Your vindication."

"What an incredible and loving God You are! "Thank You that even right now, even though I have wasted some time, I can now fix my eyes on You and receive Your provision."

Reminder: How To Meditate.

1. Study Thoughtfully.
2. Speak To Ourselves.
3. Speak To God.
4. Imagine / Picture.
5. Contemplate and Reflect.

Assignment.

1. For the next number of days, take time every day to mediate on God as your "Vindicator".

2. Ask Him to reveal to you different aspects of the fact that:

    - God vindicates us by blessing us with provision.
    - God vindicates us by humbling our enemies.
    - God vindicates us by preparing the blessing in advance.

3. Picture God standing beside you as your Shepherd in the midst of your crisis. See yourself fixing your eyes on Him. See Him stretching out His arms to you, and giving you the

provision that you need. What is He giving to you? Now see yourself receiving it.

4. Record any insights God gives you and meditate on them.

Part 16 – Knowing God As My Refresher

A Crisis Look At Psalm 23.

We are looking at Psalm 23, to help us learn how we can draw closer to God during a time of crisis.

Psalm 23:1-6, NKJV – *(1) The LORD is my shepherd; I shall not want. (2) He makes me to lie down in green pastures; He leads me beside the still waters. (3) He restores my soul; He leads me in the paths of righteousness For His name's sake. (4) Yea, though I walk through the valley of the shadow of death, I will fear no evil; For You are with me; Your rod and Your staff, they comfort me. (5) You prepare a table before me in the presence of my enemies; You anoint my head with oil; My cup runs over. (6) Surely goodness and mercy shall follow me all the days of my life; And I will dwell in the house of the LORD Forever.*

My Refresher.

1. **God Refreshes Us By Providing For Us.**

   Psalm 23:5, NIV – *(5) You <u>anoint</u> my head with oil.*

   The word “anoint” (Strong’s H1878 = דָּשֵׁן [dâshên]) means “to be fat, to fatten, to satisfy, to anoint”.

   When we face a crisis, God wants to refresh us so that we do not become discouraged or depressed or overwhelmed. One of the ways He refreshes us is by “making us fat”, by adding resources to us, by providing for our needs.

   You see, in a time of crisis our emotions can become strained, our relationships can become strained, our work environment and our home environment and our marriage can become strained, and God understands all the possible consequences if these issues are not dealt with.

So in those times, God wants us to draw close to Him, and look to Him, so that He can provide what we need, whether those needs are spiritual, physical, mental, emotional, or relational --- and usually, in a time of crisis, all five areas are effected.

Thank God for His promise to us!

Philippians 4:19, NIV – *(19) And my God will meet all your needs according to his glorious riches in Christ Jesus.*

When we experience a "leanness" due to a crisis, God comes to us and wants to "make us fat" by providing for our needs, in every area of our life.

2. God Refreshes Us By Meeting Us In Our Place Of Shaking.

Psalm 23:5, NIV – *(5) You anoint my head with oil.*

The word "head" (Strong's H7218 = ראשׁ [rô'sh]) means, literally, "to shake", or symbolically, "the head (as the part most easily shaken)".

Although the Hebrew word translated as "head" can mean "our physical head", its primary meaning is "shaking". So, when we face shaking, when we are shaken by a crisis, God comes to us in our place of shaking, to be with us, and to minister to us in that place of shaking, and give us what we need.

When we face any shaking, any challenge, any crisis in our lives, we can be sure that God is right there with us. He was with Daniel in the Lion's den, and gave him protection. He was with the disciples in the storm, and gave them peace. He was with Paul on the ship in the Mediterranean Sea, and gave him courage. And He will be with us in our time of shaking – if we invite Him.

Jesus said,

Hebrews 13:5, NIV – *(5) … "Never will I leave you; never will I forsake you."*

Matthew 28:20, NIV – *(20) … And surely I am with you always, to the very end of the age."*

Did you ever experience as a child, a time when you suddenly felt alone? Maybe you were outside in the dark, and you lost sight of your parents. Or maybe you were inside, in a large, crowded shopping mall, and you suddenly lost sight of your parents. What happened? Fear, anxiety, worry, panic, terror, dread?

And then you caught a glimpse of one of your parents, or maybe you heard one of their voices. And what happened? Suddenly the fear, anxiety, worry, panic, terror, and dread just vanished, and you were refreshed simply by the knowledge that you were not alone.

In the midst of a crisis, God wants to refresh us, and help us get rid of all of our fear, by letting us know that He is with us, in our place of shaking. And He wants to meet with us, and speak to us, and calm all of our fears with His voice and His presence.

3. God Refreshes Us By Tangibly Touching Us.

Psalm 23:5, NIV – *(5) You anoint my head with oil.*

The word "oil" (Strong's H8081 = שֶׁמֶן [shemen]) means "grease, perfumed oil or liquid, anointing".

When someone rubs us with grease, or pours oil on us – especially perfumed oil, we know it right away. How do we know it? We know it because we can feel the grease or oil on our skin, and we can smell the perfume.

And that experience will last for a period of time. The feeling of the oil may last for hours, and that smell of perfume may also last for hours, or even days. It will not be just a momentary experience, there will be a lasting effect.

God says that when we experience a crisis, He wants us to actually encounter Him – to have an experiential encounter with Him. He wants to tangibly touch us. And He doesn't just want to just touch us for a second, He wants His touch to impact us, and linger with us, so in the hours and days to come, we will still feel the effects of our encounter with Him.

Mark 5:28-29, NIV – *(28) … she thought, "If I just touch his clothes, I will be healed." (29) Immediately her bleeding stopped and she felt in her body that she was freed from her suffering.*

When the woman with the blood disorder touched the hem of Jesus' garment, even though the touch was just for a second, the effect of that touch lasted the rest of her life. An encounter with Jesus always has an enduring effect.

Romans 5:5, NIV – *(5) … God has poured out his love into our hearts by the Holy Spirit, whom he has given us.*

When we receive the Holy Spirit, the love of God is poured into our hearts in a second, but that experience of love can last a lifetime.

1 Timothy 1:14, NIV – *(14) The grace of our Lord was poured out on me abundantly, along with the faith and love that are in Christ Jesus.*

When Paul had an encounter with Jesus, God poured out His grace abundantly on Paul, and it lasted a lifetime.

And when we face a crisis, if we call out to God, He does not just come and give us a light and momentary touch – a feel-good touch that lasts for a few seconds or minutes.

Instead, He pours out His grace, and smears us with His grace, and fills us with the incense of His grace, so that we can experience His tangible touch, and enjoy the ongoing effects of that touch.

He refreshes us by allowing us to experience His tangible touch!

Prayer.

"Father, help me to allow You to be my refresher."

"Help me to know that when I face shaking, You will refresh me by providing for me. Help me to know that when I face shaking, You will meet me in my place of shaking, and be right there with me. And help me to know that when I face shaking, You will allow me to experience your tangible touch, to give me what I need in that moment, and for the months and years to come."

"What an incredible and loving God You are! Thank You that even right now, even though I may be experiencing a great shaking, just one touch from You changes everything."

Reminder: How To Meditate.

1. Study Thoughtfully.
2. Speak To Ourselves.
3. Speak To God.
4. Imagine / Picture.
5. Contemplate and Reflect.

Assignment.

1. For the next number of days, take time every day to mediate on God as your "Refresher".

2. Ask Him to reveal to you different aspects of the fact that:

    - God refreshes us by providing for us.
    - God refreshes us by meeting us in our place of shaking.
    - God refreshes us by tangibly touching us.

3. Picture God coming to you in your time of shaking. See Him lovingly placing His hands on your head, and then see Him pouring onto your head His love, His power, His healing, His courage, or whatever grace from Him you need for the days and months to come. Feel the "anointing" pouring down over your body, and feel His grace working a change in your life.

4. Record any insights God gives you and meditate on them.

Part 17 – Knowing God As My Satisfier.

A Crisis Look At Psalm 23.

We are looking at Psalm 23, to help us learn how we can draw closer to God during a time of crisis.

Psalm 23:1-6, NKJV – *(1) The LORD is my shepherd; I shall not want. (2) He makes me to lie down in green pastures; He leads me beside the still waters. (3) He restores my soul; He leads me in the paths of righteousness For His name's sake. (4) Yea, though I walk through the valley of the shadow of death, I will fear no evil; For You are with me; Your rod and Your staff, they comfort me. (5) You prepare a table before me in the presence of my enemies; You anoint my head with oil; My cup runs over. (6) Surely goodness and mercy shall follow me All the days of my life; And I will dwell in the house of the LORD Forever.*

My Satisfier.

1. **God Satisfies Us By Filling Us To Overflow.**

   Psalm 23:5, NIV – *(5) My cup runs over.*

   The phrase “runs over” (Strong’s H7310 = רְוָיָה [revâyâh]) means “receive satisfaction, runs over, makes wealthy”.

   Satisfaction.

   The first meaning of the phrase “Runs Over”, is “to receive and experience satisfaction”. The word “satisfaction” means to experience the enjoyment of having our need fully met. When we drink, we drink until our thirst is quenched, and then we are satisfied. When we eat, we eat until our hunger is gone, and then we are satisfied. When we are satisfied, we are not left needing and longing for more.

When God gives to us, He does not just give us a very small portion, so that after we receive it, we are still in a place of need. When God meets one of our needs, He meets that need fully.

It may come in a "lump sum", or in a series of provisions, but He WILL meet our need fully. He may give us new avenues of provision to pursue, but He promises to satisfy us – to fully meet our needs.

If God is our Shepherd, He satisfies us – He fully meets our needs.

Isaiah 58:11, NIV – *(11) The LORD will guide you always; he will satisfy your needs in a sun-scorched land and will strengthen your frame. …*

When God is our Shepherd, even in a time of crisis, God will meet and satisfy our needs.

Overflow.

The second meaning of the phrase "Runs Over", is "to be completely filled, and then overflowing", so that there will always be a God-induced overflowing out of our lives.

When God is our Shepherd, there is always an overflow.

We will never have to worry that our God-given resources will run dry, or that they will become exhausted. Yes, our human resources may be limited, but God wants us to learn to receive and minister from His overflow in our lives.

When God is our Shepherd and our source, we will become like an Artesian well, where the constant source of life-giving water keeps pushing to the surface, and enabling us to bless others out of the endless source of God's provision.

Isaiah 58:11, NIV – *(11) ... You will be like a well-watered garden, like a spring whose waters never fail.*

When God is our Shepherd, there will be a constant overflow, even in a time of crisis.

Make Wealthy.

The phrase “Runs Over” also means, “to make wealthy”.

What does it mean to be wealthy? It basically means to have more than enough resources.

It means that we will have our own needs met, and we will also have some left over, so that we will be able to be generous, and share with other people, during THEIR time of crisis.

2 Corinthians 9:8, NIV – *(8) And God is able to make all grace abound to you, so that in all things at all times, having all that you need, you will abound in every good work.*

The primary definition of “God’s grace” is “God’s unmerited favour toward us”. So even during a time of crisis, God is able to make His unmerited favour abound to us, in our personal lives, in our marriages, in our business, and in our ministry, so that we will have all that we need to abound in our own lives, and also abound in every good work as we bless other people’s lives.

God will make His grace abound to us, so that through His favour, we can abound in everything we do. God wants to fill us to overflow – to make us wealthy with all the necessary resources from heaven that we need, so that we can abound in every good work that we do for Him.

2. God Satisfies Us In Our Personal Lives.

Psalm 23:5, NIV – *(5) My cup runs over.*

The word "cup" (Strong's H3563 = כּוֹס [kôs]) means "to hold together, cup or container, a lot or portion"

So, the first meaning of the word "cup" is "cup or container". Our cup or container obviously speaks of our personal lives. Our cup is our heart, soul, mind, and strength.

God our Shepherd wants to satisfy us in our personal lives, so that we would be full and overflowing with love, and joy, and peace, and so much more.

Ephesians 5:18, NIV – *(1) … be filled with the Spirit.*

Philippians 1:11, NIV – *(11) … filled with the fruit of righteousness that comes through Jesus Christ — to the glory and praise of God.*

1 Peter 1:8, NIV – *(8) … you believe in him and are filled with an inexpressible and glorious joy.*

When God is our Shepherd, we can be filled in every area of our lives, even in a time of crisis.

3. God Satisfies Us In Our Public Lives.

Psalm 23:5, NIV – *(5) My cup runs over.*

The second meaning of the word "cup" is "lot or portion". Our "lot or portion" speaks of our **public** lives.

Our lot in life, or our portion in life, is our purpose or our assignment from God, and the things that God has given to us as resources, so that we can fulfil our purpose.

Ephesians 2:10, NIV – *(10) For we are God's workmanship, created in Christ Jesus to do good works, which God prepared in advance for us to do.*

God has given each one of us a life purpose, as well as specific assignments to accomplish throughout our lives, that God prepared in advance for us to do. And as we live our lives for Him, He will bring those opportunities to us at the right time and ask us to complete our assignments for Him.

So, God will satisfy us, by filling us or giving us everything that we need, so that we can fulfill our purpose in life.

We can never argue that we cannot fulfill our purpose in life because we are lacking some ability. God has filled us with everything we need to do what we are called to do.

2 Thessalonians 1:11, NIV – *(11) ... by his power he may fulfill every good purpose of yours and every act prompted by your faith.*

Philippians 4:13, NIV – *(13) I can do everything through him who gives me strength.*

We can do everything through Christ, because He gives us the strength, and the resources to do what He has called us to do. So, we can be completely satisfied in our public life – our life in relationship with others.

Prayer.

"Father, help me to allow You to be my satisfier."

"Help me to draw close to You, so that You can satisfy me by filling me to overflow. Help me to draw close to You, so that You can satisfy me in my personal life and give me all that I need. And help me to draw close to You, so that You can satisfy me in my public life, so that I can be a source of blessing to others, in all of my relationships, and in every place where I put my feet."

"What an incredible and loving God You are! Thank You that even right now, as I reach out to You, You are satisfying me, by filling me again with Your grace and provision."

Reminder: How To Meditate.

1. Study Thoughtfully.
2. Speak To Ourselves.
3. Speak To God.
4. Imagine / Picture.
5. Contemplate and Reflect.

Assignment.

1. For the next number of days, take time every day to mediate on God as your "Satisfier".

2. Ask Him to reveal to you different aspects of the fact that:

    - God satisfies us by filling us to overflow.
    - God satisfies us in our personal lives.
    - God satisfies us in our public lives.

3. Picture yourself sitting before God, and letting God see everything you need in your personal life for this day. Now see Him pouring those things into your life, so that you experience a sense of complete satisfaction.

4. Now picture yourself sitting before God, and letting God see everything you need in your public life for this day. Now see Him pouring those things into your life, so that you can experience a sense of complete satisfaction as you serve others.

5. Record any insights God gives you and meditate on them.

Part 18 – Knowing God As My Pursuer

A Crisis Look At Psalm 23.

We are looking at Psalm 23, to help us learn how we can draw closer to God during a time of crisis.

Psalm 23:1-6, NKJV – *(1) The LORD is my shepherd; I shall not want. (2) He makes me to lie down in green pastures; He leads me beside the still waters. (3) He restores my soul; He leads me in the paths of righteousness For His name's sake. (4) Yea, though I walk through the valley of the shadow of death, I will fear no evil; For You are with me; Your rod and Your staff, they comfort me. (5) You prepare a table before me in the presence of my enemies; You anoint my head with oil; My cup runs over. (6) Surely goodness and mercy shall follow me All the days of my life; And I will dwell in the house of the LORD Forever.*

My Pursuer.

1. **God Pursues Us Passionately.**

   Psalm 23:6, NKJV - *(6) Surely goodness and mercy <u>shall follow me</u> all the days of my life;*

   The phrase “shall follow me” (Strong’s H7291 = רָדַף [râdaph]) means “to run after, to chase, to hunt, to pursue”.

   God is not just **FOLLOWING** us with grace and mercy, He is **PURSUING** us, running after us, chasing us, hunting after us, in order to bless us with His goodness and mercy.

   Many people tend to have the idea that God the Judge is sitting in heaven, just waiting for us to perform well enough to get His attention. We think that if we beg Him enough, or weep enough, or wail enough, or promise Him enough, or sacrifice for Him enough, then He will consider meeting our needs. How far from the truth!

The truth is, that as our Shepherd and our loving Father, He is pursuing us – He is chasing after us, in order to bless us!

In fact, He has already provided for us everything we need.

2 Peter 1:3, NIV – *(3) His divine power has given us everything we need for life and godliness through our knowledge of him who called us by his own glory and goodness.*

To Receive His Resources.

If God has already given us everything we need for life and godliness, then why is He pursuing us? He is pursuing us, because He wants us to slow down, so that we will take the time to receive what He has given us.

Most of us act like we are in a relay racing, running faster and faster so that we can win the prize for the sake of our team. But God is like the runner behind us, who has the baton to pass on to us, and we cannot win the race without His baton.

So He is calling out to us to slow down a bit, so that we can receive His baton – His resources for our life – without dropping it, so that we can run with all of His resources and actually finish and win the race.

To Pull Down His Blessings.

Ephesians 1:3, NIV – *(3) Praise be to the God and Father of our Lord Jesus Christ, who has blessed us in the heavenly realms with every spiritual blessing in Christ.*

The second reason that God is pursuing us, is because all of our spiritual blessings are stored up for us in heaven – in the heavenly realms, and He is pursuing us so that we will learn how to pull down those blessings from the heavenly realm, and into the earthly realm.

Although God has given us everything we need, we need to learn how to pull them down, so that they become manifest in the earthly realm.

Many Christians get to the end of their lives with the largest amount of their blessings still sitting for them in a heavenly vault, because they have never learned how to open the vault, and pull down those resources to earth, and receive those blessings into their lives.

God is pursuing us passionately, to teach us how to receive them.

2. **God Pursues Us Constantly.**

Psalm 23:6, NKJV - *(6) Surely goodness and mercy shall follow me all the days of my life.*

The word “all” (Strong’s H3605 = כֹּל [kôl]) means “the whole, all, any and every, altogether”.

The word “days” (Strong’s H3117 = יוֹם [yôm]) means “days, age, continually, perpetually, from sundown to sundown”.

So, God is pursuing us daily, each and every day, and throughout the whole of our lives.

God does not take a holiday – He pursues us every day, from the day we are born, until the day we die. And God does not get tired – He does not need to rest from pursuing us, even though some of us may make it difficult for Him to catch us.

And God does not pursue us conditionally, so that if we do good enough, or pray enough, or behave well enough, then He may decide to pursue us. No, God pursues us each and every day, no matter what is happening in our lives.

And God does not pursue only on select days. God does not say, "Oh, it is the first Thursday of the month – today is the day I pursue that person". No, God pursues us each and every day.

And God does not pursue us only during the day. He pursues us from sundown to sundown, meaning He pursues us during the day, and during the night. He pursues us when we are awake, and He pursues us when we are asleep. Yes, He pursues us, even in our dreams!

God is always pursuing us, to bless us.

Psalm 139:7-10, NIV – *(7) Where can I go from your Spirit? Where can I flee from your presence? (8) If I go up to the heavens, you are there; if I make my bed in the depths, you are there. (9) If I rise on the wings of the dawn, if I settle on the far side of the sea, (10) even there your hand will guide me, your right hand will hold me fast.*

God is indeed our pursuer, and He consistently purses us, in order to bless us.

Prayer.

"Father, help me to allow You to be my pursuer."

"Help me to realize that You pursue me passionately, because You desire so much to bless me. And help me to realize that

You pursue me constantly, so that I can always have confidence, that no matter what is going on in my life, You are right here with me, to take care of me.

"What an incredible and loving God You are! Thank You that even right now, You are pursuing me, to bless me, and protect me, even in this time of crisis."

Reminder: How To Meditate.

1. Study Thoughtfully.
2. Speak To Ourselves.
3. Speak To God.
4. Imagine / Picture.
5. Contemplate and Reflect.

Assignment.

1. For the next number of days, take time every day to mediate on God as your "Pursuer".

2. Ask Him to reveal to you different aspects of the fact that:

   - God pursues us passionately.
   - God pursues us constantly.

3. Close your eyes and imagine yourself running down a street. Now, look around you, and see that God is right behind you, pursuing you, with a large parcel of blessing in His hands. Take the time to stop, turn to Him, and receive His parcel of blessing for you. What is He giving you?

4. Record any insights God gives you and meditate on them.

Part 19 – Knowing God As My Kindness-Shower

A Crisis Look At Psalm 23.

We are looking at Psalm 23, to help us learn how we can draw closer to God during a time of crisis.

Psalm 23:1-6, NKJV – *(1) The LORD is my shepherd; I shall not want. (2) He makes me to lie down in green pastures; He leads me beside the still waters. (3) He restores my soul; He leads me in the paths of righteousness For His name's sake. (4) Yea, though I walk through the valley of the shadow of death, I will fear no evil; For You are with me; Your rod and Your staff, they comfort me. (5) You prepare a table before me in the presence of my enemies; You anoint my head with oil; My cup runs over. (6) Surely goodness and mercy shall follow me All the days of my life; And I will dwell in the house of the LORD Forever.*

My Kindness-Shower.

Psalm 23:6, NKJV - *(6) Surely goodness and mercy shall follow me all the days of my life.*

Last time we learned that God is passionately and consistently pursuing us to bless us. But what, specifically, is God wanting to bless us with? Two things – goodness and mercy.

Now, what are goodness and mercy?

The word “goodness” (Strong’s H2896 = טוֹב [ṭôb]) means “goodness, bountifulness, favour, graciousness, kindness, wealth, welfare”.

So, God's GOODNESS seems to be all sorts of blessings that God wants to GIVE us, that we certainly DO NOT deserve, like favour, and grace, and wealth, and welfare -- simply because He loves us.

The word "mercy" (Strong's H3117 = חֶסֶד [chêsêd]) means "kindness, mercy, pity, good deeds, withholding reproof or reproach".

God's MERCY seems to be all sorts of punishment and negative things that God wants to WITHHOLD from us, that we certainly DO deserve, like reproof and reproach – because of our sinfulness.

So God's GOODNESS is God showing us kindness, by giving us what we DO NOT deserve – His blessings, and God's MERCY is God showing us kindness, by NOT giving us what we DO deserve – His punishment.

1. **God Is Kind To Us By Showing Us His Mercy.**

First, let us look at God's Mercy.

God's Mercy Is Better Than Man's.

2 Samuel 24:14, NIV – *(14) .... Let us <u>fall into the hands of the LORD</u>, for <u>his mercy is great</u>; but do not let me fall into the hands of men."*

No matter how much we have failed, God's mercy is so much better than any mercy we can ever experience at the hands of men.

God's Mercy Is Great.

Nehemiah 9:31, NIV – *(31) But in <u>your great mercy</u> you did not put an end to them or abandon them, for you are a gracious and merciful God.*

We do not have to worry that God may be having a bad day, and so His mercy will be less than yesterday. God's mercy is always great.

God's Mercy Is Everlasting

Psalm 25:6, NIV – *(6) Remember, O LORD, your great mercy and love, for they are from of old.*

God's mercy is from of old, meaning that God's mercy has always existed, and always will exist. God's mercy is everlasting.

God's Mercy Is Guaranteed.

Isaiah 55:7, NIV – *(7) Let the wicked forsake his way and the evil man his thoughts. Let him turn to the LORD, and he will have mercy on him, and to our God, for he will freely pardon.*

If we forsake our evil ways and our evil thoughts, God's mercy is guaranteed. God WILL have mercy on us.

God's Mercy Is Completely Undeserved.

Ephesians 2:4-5, NIV – *(4) But because of his great love for us, God, who is rich in mercy, (5) made us alive with Christ even when we were dead in transgressions — it is by grace you have been saved.*

Even though we did not deserve it at all, even before we even thought about dealing with our sins, God showed us His great mercy, and made us alive with Christ. This is the type of mercy that God pursues us with, each and every day.

2. God Is Kind To Us By Showing Us His Goodness.

Now let us look at God's goodness.

God's Goodness Causes Him To Intervene On Our Behalf.

Genesis 50:20, NIV – *(20) You intended to harm me, but God intended it for good to accomplish what is now being done, the saving of many lives.*

God is so great in His goodness, that it motivates Him to turn every challenge into a blessing. Even when we mess up – we make mistakes – God wants to turn all of our failures into something good for us.

God's Goodness Causes Him To Make Us Wonderful Promises.

1 Chronicles 17:26, NIV – *(26) O LORD, you are God! You have promised these good things to your servant.*

Whenever God makes a promise to us, we can be sure that all of His promises are good for us, so we can take Him at His word, and trust Him.

God's Goodness Causes Him To Plan A Good Purpose For Our Lives.

Philippians 2:13, NIV – *(13) for it is God who works in you to will and to act according to his good purpose.*

Because of God's goodness, He has created us with a good purpose, and then He works in us by His Spirit – in our desires and our actions – to move us to fulfill that purpose.

God's Goodness Causes Him To Provide For Us.

1 Timothy 4:4, NIV – *(4) For everything God created is good, and nothing is to be rejected if it is received with thanksgiving,*

Everything God creates is good, and so even when we are in a crisis, in a time we need, we can be sure that God will create something good for us, to provide for us, and so we can always receive it with thanksgiving.

God's Goodness Causes Him To Discipline Us For Our Good.

Hebrews 12:10, NIV – *(10) Our fathers disciplined us for a little while as they thought best; but God disciplines us for our good, that we may share in his holiness.*

No matter how much we mess up – no matter how severe our mistakes – we can be sure that if God disciplines us, it will be for our good. He will not discipline us to hurt us or to punish us, but to purify us.

So, each and every day, God pursues us, in order to demonstrate His mercy and His goodness to us. In His MERCY, He DOES NOT give us the things that we DO deserve – our punishment, and in His GOODNESS, He DOES give us the things that we DO NOT deserve – His blessings.

What a great God we serve!

As David the Psalmist said:

Psalm 116:12, NIV – *(12) How can I repay the LORD for all his goodness to me?*

Prayer.

"Father, help me to allow You to be my Kindness-Shower."

"Help me to realize that You are merciful, and You DO NOT give me those things that I deserve, like punishment for all of my sins and failures. And help me to realize that You are merciful, and You DO give me those things that I DO NOT deserve, like all of Your blessings to me."

"And thank You that even in a time of crisis, even when I may be at my very worst, You are always at Your very best, and You will pursue me with Your mercy and Your goodness."

Reminder: How To Meditate.

1. Study Thoughtfully.
2. Speak To Ourselves.
3. Speak To God.
4. Imagine / Picture.
5. Contemplate and Reflect.

Assignment.

1. For the next number of days, take time every day to mediate on God as your "Kindness-Shower".

2. Ask Him to reveal to you different aspects of the fact that:

   - God is merciful, and He does not give us those things that we do deserve, like judgement and punishment.
   - God is good, and He does give us those things that we do not deserve, like all of the great blessings that He has for us.

3. Picture yourself in a place of recent failure. See God coming to do in your time of shame and throwing away any rod of punishment that may have been placed at your feet.

See Him instead embracing you and pouring His love and forgiveness and comfort and healing and strength into your life. What is He saying to you as He ministers to you?

4. Record any insights God gives you and meditate on them.

Part 20 – Knowing God As My Dwelling Place

A Crisis Look At Psalm 23.

We are looking at Psalm 23, to help us learn how we can draw closer to God during a time of crisis.

Psalm 23:1-6, NKJV – *(1) The LORD is my shepherd; I shall not want. (2) He makes me to lie down in green pastures; He leads me beside the still waters. (3) He restores my soul; He leads me in the paths of righteousness For His name's sake. (4) Yea, though I walk through the valley of the shadow of death, I will fear no evil; For You are with me; Your rod and Your staff, they comfort me. (5) You prepare a table before me in the presence of my enemies; You anoint my head with oil; My cup runs over. (6) Surely goodness and mercy shall follow me All the days of my life; And I will dwell in the house of the LORD Forever.*

My Dwelling Place.

> Psalm 23:6, NIV - *(6) … And I will dwell in the house of the LORD Forever.*

1. An Abiding Place.

The word “dwell” (Strong’s H3427 = יָשַׁב [yâshab]) means “to sit down, to dwell, to remain, to settle, to abide”.

So, the “house of the Lord” is not like a hotel, where we stop for a short rest. It is not like a cottage, where we just go for a week or two. And it is not like a house, where we only spend our evenings and nights. Instead, it is a place, or a state of being, that we can remain in, and abide in, all the time.

2. A Place Of Safety And Provision.

The word “house” (Strong’s H1004 = בַּיִת [bayith]) means “a house, a home, a palace”.

“The house of the Lord” is not just a house, that we can live in. It is more like a home, where we can feel safe and secure. But it is also like a palace, where there is sufficient provision for all of our needs to be met. There is no lack inside a palace!

3. A Place Of Continual Experience.

The word “forever” (Strong’s H753 + H3117 = אֹרֶךְ ['ôrek] + יוֹם [yôm]) means “each and every day forever”.

So even in a time of crisis, if we allow God to be our Shepherd, there is a dwelling place, a state of being that we can abide in, each and every day of our lives – today, tomorrow, and for all eternity.

Our dwelling place is NOT a place that we will one day go to. Our dwelling place is a place that we can experience today, and learn to abide there, each and every day throughout our earthly life, and then into eternity.

This promise was revealed to us through the Psalmist David, and was reconfirmed by Jesus, the Son of God.

The Power Of Our Dwelling Place.

So, what can we learn about “The house of the Lord” – our God-given home, our abiding place, our eternal dwelling place – according to the New Testament?

1. **Our Dwelling Place Must Be Jesus.**

John 15:4, NIV – *(4) Remain in me, and I will remain in you. No branch can bear fruit by itself; it must remain in the vine. Neither can you bear fruit unless you remain in me.*

First and foremost, our dwelling place is to be in Jesus. We will never have a secure home for our lives outside of Jesus. He is to be our dwelling place, and from that dwelling place, we will be able to bear much fruit.

Although we are one day promised a room in heaven, we must first make sure that our eternal dwelling place, and especially our dwelling place here on earth, is in Jesus. He is our dwelling place, our life source, and the source of all of our fruitfulness.

And even in a time of crisis, we can experience this dwelling place NOW, and we can experience His life NOW, and we can experience fruitfulness NOW.

2. **Our Dwelling Place Determines Our Rest.**

Matthew 11:28, NIV – *(28) "Come to me, all you who are weary and burdened, and I will give you rest."*

Hebrews 4:1, NIV – *(1) Therefore, since the promise of entering his rest still stands, let us be careful that none of you be found to have fallen short of it.*

Jesus said that if we come to Him, that He would give us rest. But that rest is not attained by just hanging out with Jesus. That rest is attained by making Him our dwelling place, so that we can experience the promise of "entering into" His rest.

There is a big difference between "resting", and "entering into rest". "Resting" means we strive hard, then we take a break, then we strive hard, then we take a break.

"Entering into rest" means that we abide in a state of rest, and everything we do, we do from a place of rest, where there is no striving.

When Jesus is our dwelling place, we can abide in a place of eternal rest.

3. Our Dwelling Place Determines Our Fruitfulness.

John 15:5-6, NIV – *(5) "I am the vine; you are the branches. If a man remains in me and I in him, he will bear much fruit; apart from me you can do nothing.(6) If anyone does not remain in me, he is like a branch that is thrown away and withers; such branches are picked up, thrown into the fire and burned.*

Jesus said that if we make Him our dwelling place, we will bear much fruit. But if we do not make Him our dwelling place, we will become like a dried-up old stick that is useful for nothing but firewood.

Many people think, "Yes, I know, Jesus wants to be my dwelling place, my abiding place, and so when I get through this crisis – when I get some time – I will learn how to make Him my dwelling place, because I realize that if I make Him my dwelling place, then I can finally experience some rest in my life."

However, they are completely missing the point. Unless Jesus is our dwelling place, not only will we NOT experience real rest, we will also NOT experience real life, and so our fruit will be minimal or even non-existent. And being void of His life, we will just wither up.

It is NOW, during this time of crisis, that we need to make Jesus our dwelling place. If we do, we can be fruitful, even NOW in the midst of this crisis, and continue to produce fruit, even after this crisis is over.

4. Our Dwelling Place Determines Our Provision.

John 15:7, NIV – *(7) If you remain in me and my words remain in you, ask whatever you wish, and it will be given you.*

Jesus said that if we abide in Him, if we make our dwelling place in Him, then from our dwelling place, we can ask Him to meet all of our needs, and they will be given to us.

Our dwelling place is not just a place of rest and protection, our dwelling place is a place of provision. It is a place where, no matter what is going on around us, we can live in confidence, knowing that when we are in our dwelling place, we can ask God and be confident that He will meet our needs.

So, in a time of crisis, it is imperative that we make Jesus our dwelling place, so that we can receive all of the provision that we need for our lives.

Prayer.

“Father, help me to allow You to be my Dwelling Place.”

“Help me to realize that it is only in Jesus, that I experience my dwelling place. Help me to realize that when Jesus is my dwelling place, I can experience real rest. Help me to realize that when Jesus is my dwelling place, I can produce real and lasting fruit. And help me to realize that when Jesus is my dwelling place, all of my needs will be provided for.”

“What an incredible and loving God You are! Thank You that even right now, in the middle of a crisis, I can find my dwelling place in You, and experience rest, and fruitfulness, and provision, both right now, and for all of eternity.”

Reminder: How To Meditate.

1. Study Thoughtfully.
2. Speak To Ourselves.
3. Speak To God.
4. Imagine / Picture.
5. Contemplate and Reflect.

Assignment.

1. For the next number of days, take time every day to mediate on God as your “Dwelling Place”.

2. Ask Him to reveal to you different aspects of the fact that:

    - Our dwelling place is Jesus.
    - Our dwelling place determines our rest.
    - Our dwelling place determines our fruitfulness.
    - Our dwelling place determines our provision.

3. Picture yourself, right now, sitting before Jesus. See Him open His arms up to you and embrace you. Now make the choice to stay in His arms.

4. Now see yourself going to work tomorrow, with His arms still embracing you, so that you will experience His rest, fruitfulness, and provision throughout the day.

5. Now see yourself going through a challenging time, with His arms still embracing you, so that you can experience His rest, fruitfulness, and provision in that challenging time.

6. Now, no matter what you do for the rest of this day, try to picture His arms still embracing you, and learn how to live with Him as your Dwelling Place.

7. Record any insights God gives you and meditate on them.

Part 21 – Knowing God As My Speaker

A Crisis Look At Psalm 23.

Let us look at Psalm 23 one more time.

Psalm 23:1-6, NKJV – *(1) The LORD is my shepherd; I shall not want. (2) He makes me to lie down in green pastures; He leads me beside the still waters. (3) He restores my soul; He leads me in the paths of righteousness For His name's sake. (4) Yea, though I walk through the valley of the shadow of death, I will fear no evil; For You are with me; Your rod and Your staff, they comfort me. (5) You prepare a table before me in the presence of my enemies; You anoint my head with oil; My cup runs over. (6) Surely goodness and mercy shall follow me All the days of my life; And I will dwell in the house of the LORD Forever.*

1. **Letting God Reveal Himself To Us.**

   We started this series by saying that we needed to be like the men of Issachar, who knew what to do in their time of crisis. And we agreed that what WE need to do during THIS time of crisis, is to draw close to God.

   Over the last number of lessons, we have been meditating on Psalm 23, which is usually a Psalm read only at funerals, but we discovered that it is also a great Psalm to look at during a time of crisis to help us draw close to God, especially if we meditate on it.

   And what did we discover in every verse, as we meditated on it? In every verse we discovered some aspect of **God's Nature** or **God's Character!**

   We discovered that God is **our Lord, our Shepherd,** and **our Provider.**

We discovered that God is **our Rest-Giver, our Guide,** and **our Restorer.**

We discovered that God is **our Protector, our Courage-Giver,** and **our Comforter.**

We discovered that God is **our Vindicator, our Refresher,** and **our Satisfier.**

We discovered that God is **our Pursuer, our Kindness-Shower,** and **our Dwelling Place.**

And hopefully, as we mediated on Psalm 23, we discovered even more aspects of the nature and character of God.

You see, this is the real key to drawing close to God – simply to spend time with Him and discover who He really is. Actually, this is the key to drawing close to anyone – to first spend time with them and discover who they really are, not who we THINK they are, or who someone else may have told us they are.

To draw close to my wife, I do not need to just let others tell me who she is and what she is like. And I do not need to make my own assumptions about who she is, so that I develop a better "theology" about my wife, or more accurately, a better "wifeology".

Instead, I just need to spend time with her, and let her reveal to me who she really is.

And so if we are going to draw close to God, we must spend time with Him, and let Him reveal to us who He really is, and as we discover who He really is, we will begin to trust Him more, and learn better how to receive His love and His provision for us, even in a time of crisis.

2. Listening To God's Voice.

But if we are going to spend time with God and let Him reveal to us who He really is, there is one more thing that we must do – we must learn to listen to His voice.

John 10:27, NIV – *(27) My sheep listen to my voice; I know them, and they follow me.*

Jesus said, "My sheep listen to my voice." If God is our Shepherd, then we are His sheep, and so, if we are His sheep, and His sheep listen to His voice, we MUST take time to listen to His voice.

Moses was in a place of a crisis, a place of desperation, because the Israelites were resisting his leadership, and so Moses sought God, and asked God for His help and His wisdom. And then Moses cried out to God:

Exodus 33:18, NIV – *(18) Then Moses said, "Now show me your glory."*

Now, I am not sure if Moses really even realized what He was asking for, because **God's glory is the revelation and demonstration of His nature and His character – who He is and what He is like.**

How did God respond?

Exodus 33:19, NIV – *(19) And the LORD said, "I will cause all my goodness to pass in front of you, and I will proclaim my name, the LORD, in your presence. ...*

Moses asked to see God's glory, and God responded, "I will show you My goodness, and proclaim My name".

So, what happened next? God put Moses in a place of safety, in the cleft of a rock, and He revealed His nature and character to Moses.

Exodus 34:5-7, NIV – *(5) Then the LORD came down in the cloud and stood there with him and proclaimed his name, the LORD. (6) And he passed in front of Moses, proclaiming, "The LORD, the LORD, the compassionate and gracious God, slow to anger, abounding in love and faithfulness, (7) maintaining love to thousands, and forgiving wickedness, rebellion and sin. Yet he does not leave the guilty unpunished …*

Moses asked to see God's glory. God responded by declaring to Moses – by SPEAKING to Moses and telling Moses about His nature and character – His compassion, His graciousness, His love, His faithfulness, and His justice.

So, if we are going to draw close to God in a time of crisis, we must **spend TIME with God**, and **MEDIATE on His word**, AND … **LISTEN to His voice.**

3. **Hearing God's Voice.**

So how did God reveal His glory to Moses? He SPOKE to Moses, and declared Who He was, and Moses listened, and HEARD His voice.

Romans 10:17, NKJV – *(17) So then <u>faith comes by hearing</u>, and hearing by <u>the word</u> of God.*

The word "faith" (Strong's G4102 = πίστις [pistis]) means "faith, persuasion, conviction of truth, reliance, assurance, belief".

So, if we want to have faith in God – meaning to trust Him, and rely on Him, especially in a time of crisis – we must hear the word of God.

However, the word "word" used here (Strong's G4487 = ῥῆμα [rhēma]) means "the utterance, the saying, the speaking". It is not the "written word" (the Logos), it is the "spoken word" (the rhema).

So the way to draw close to God is to spend TIME with Him, and MEDIATE on His word, and LISTEN to Him as He speaks to us, so that what He says goes deep into our hearts, and it becomes faith, assurance, conviction, reliance and trust in Him.

So when I mediate on the fact that God is my provider, I don't just say it to myself, I must then stop, quiet myself, and then ask God to speak to me that He is my provider. Then I wait silently, as He speaks to me, and tells me that He is my provider, and God's spoken word quickens my spirit.

When I mediate on the fact that God is my Rest-Giver, I don't just say it to myself, I must then stop, quiet myself, and ask God to speak to me that He is my Rest-Giver. Then I wait silently, as He speaks to me, and tells me that He is my rest-giver, and God's spoken word quickens my spirit.

And as I learn to do that, His voice goes beyond my mind – it goes deep down into my heart and my spirit, and very quickly I experience my faith and assurance and trust in God growing to even greater levels, and then I am better able to draw close to God, and trust Him, even in a time of crisis.

Whatever I need to have faith for, to trust God for, I must meditate on it, declare it to God, and then listen to the voice of God, as He speaks it back to me, right into my heart and spirit.

And then I will draw even more close to God, and be able to trust Him even more, even in a time of crisis.

Prayer.

“Father, help me to take the time to listen to You, and hear Your voice.”

“As I meditate on Who You are, on Your nature and character, help me to declare it to be true, but then also help me to hear You declare it to me, so that Who You are goes deep into my soul and spirit, so that I can trust You, fully, even in a time of crisis.”

“What an incredible and loving God You are! You not only want me to learn who You are, so that I can trust You fully, You also want to speak to me, so that Your voice, resonating in my spirit and my soul, results in a total reliance on You, no matter what is going on around me.”

“Thank You, God, for Your great grace toward me. In Jesus' name, Amen!”

Reminder: How To Meditate.

1. Study Thoughtfully.
2. Speak To Ourselves.
3. Speak To God.
4. Imagine / Picture.
5. Contemplate and Reflect.

Assignment.

1. For the next few days and months (or better yet – for the rest of your life), spend TIME with God, each and every

day. MEDIATE on His word, and then sit quiet and still before Him, and invite Him to SPEAK His word into your spirit and your soul.

2. Allow His speaking to build conviction, assurance, faith, and trust into your life, and thank Him for taking the time to speak to you, as His son or daughter.

3. If you need more help in hearing the voice of God, take my course "How To Hear God's Voice", or purchase my book on Amazon.[4]

---

[4] https://www.amazon.ca/How-Hear-Gods-Voice-Clarity-ebook/dp/B07FBDW9M1/

Resources To Help You Draw Close To God

Use these resources to inspire you and to help you as you endeavour to draw closer to God and hear His voice.

Feel free to click on the footnote links and check out additional resources.

The Attributes Of God

To assist you as you endeavour to draw close to God, below is a partial list of some of the many attributes of God. Feel free to spend TIME with God every day, read one verse, MEDIATE on it, and then listen as God SPEAKS His nature and character back to you.

Feel free to add to this list, as you discover new verses about God's nature and character!

1. God is Infinite – Colossians 1:17.
2. God is Unchangeable (Immutable) – Malachi 3:6.
3. God is Self-Sufficient – John 5:26.
4. God is All-Powerful (Omnipotent) – Psalm 33:6.
5. God is All-Knowing (Omniscient) – Isaiah 46:9-10.
6. God is Always Everywhere (Omnipresent) – Psalm 139:7-10.
7. God is All-Wise – Romans 11:33.
8. God is Faithful – Deuteronomy 7:9.
9. God is Good – Psalm 34:8.
10. God is Just – Deuteronomy 32:4.
11. God is Merciful – Romans 9:15-16.
12. God Is Gracious – Psalm 145:8.
13. God Is Loving and Is Love – 1 John 4:7-8.
14. God is Holy (Perfect) – Revelation 4:8.
15. God is Glorious – Habakkuk 3:4.

Letter From God To Man[5]

This letter is many Bible Promises from God to you. Read the Bible as if was written to you, because it was.[6]

To My precious child:

Because I knew even before I created the earth that you would accept My love for you, and that you would seek to know Me thus…

In the beginning I created the heavens and the earth. Then at the right time and in the right place I created you. I created your inner most being, I created every part of you, I knit you together in your mother's womb. You were carefully and wonderfully made; my works are wonderful, and you My precious child are my work. My eyes saw your unformed body. All the days planned for you were written in my book before one of them came to be. How precious are my thoughts for you, How great is the number of them! If you were to count them, they would outnumber the grains of sand.

Listen to me, My precious child; I created you and have cared for you since before you were born. I will be your God throughout your lifetime, until your hair is white with age. I made you, and I will care for you. I will carry you along and save you. I will carry you in my arms, holding you close to my heart. For I know the plans that I have for you plans to prosper you and not to harm you, plans to give you hope and a future.

My precious child, there are some times of suffering in your life. But the temporary suffering of this life does not compare to the glory that shall be revealed in you. Know this that I am with you and I will help you. Your help comes from me, I am the God who created the heavens and the earth, and the one

[5] https://god.net/the-letter-from-god/

who created you. I will never leave you, I will never reject you. When your parents fail you, I will pick you up, hold you close, and adopt you. Nothing can ever separate you from my love for you. When you are in trouble and distress my love is with you. When you are persecuted my love is with you. When you are hungry and cold and naked my love is with you, I am always with you. When you are in danger and threatened with death my love is with you, I will be with you forever.

My precious child know that nothing can separate you from my love, no matter how high you go, no matter how deep you sink, nothing in life and not even death can separate you from Me, and My love for you. No demon or any other power in hell can separate you from my love. My love for you is revealed through Christ Jesus your Lord. In all things and every situation, you will have victory, you will conquer, because the victory of Christ Jesus is your victory.

But now, My precious child, I the LORD, who created you and formed you, says: Do not be afraid, for I have purchased you. I have called you by name; you are mine. When you go through deep waters and great trouble, I will be with you. When you go through rivers of difficulty, they will not over flow you. When you walk through the fire, you will not be burned. I command you to be strong and courageous! Do not be afraid; do not be dismayed, for I, the LORD your God will be with you everywhere you go.

My precious child, know that everything will work together for your good, because you love me. You have been called according to my purpose. For I knew you before you were born and I predestined you to be conformed to the likeness of my Son, Jesus Christ. This is your destiny, and this is your purpose, that you become one with my Son Jesus, and thus one with me. I created you in my image so that you and I can express love to each other. The most intimate relationship you can have is with me because you and I are becoming one. You and your brothers and sisters that believe in me are becoming one with Jesus, and thus one with me. You in me, and me in you, together, unified by my love for you. You were designed for this purpose, nothing else will ever satisfy your deepest needs, your deepest desires, only I can. Because you seek to know me, I satisfy your heart with love, joy, and peace that only I can give you.

My precious child if you should forget me, and enter into sin, and not turn back to Me on your own then I will punish you. Because your sin will separate you from feeling My presence, and My influence, and I want you to return to your first love, the One who loves you. I the Lord discipline those I love, and I punish everyone who I accept as my child. Just as a good Father disciplines His children to turn them away from a dangerous path, so I shall discipline you for your good, that you may share in My holiness. No discipline seems pleasant at the time, but painful. Later on, however, it produces a harvest of righteousness and peace for those who have been trained by it.

My precious child, When you confess your sins, I am faithful and just and will forgive you of your sins and cleanse you from all unrighteousness. In repentance and resting in Me is your salvation, in quietness and trusting Me is your strength. I will create in you a clean heart and renew a right spirit within you. I will not send you away from My presence, and I will not take My Holy Spirit from you. I will restore again the joy of your salvation, and make you willing to obey Me. Then you will teach My ways to sinners, and they will return to Me also. Humble yourself, therefore, under My mighty hand, that I may lift you up at the right time.

My precious child, do not forget all my benefits. I forgive all your sins and heal all your diseases; I rescue your life from the pit of destruction and crown you with love and compassion. I satisfy your desires with good things so that your youth is renewed like the eagles. I The LORD work righteousness and justice for all the oppressed; I The LORD am compassionate and gracious, slow to anger, abounding in love. I will not always accuse, nor will I harbor my anger forever; I do not treat you as your sins deserve or repay you according to your iniquities. For as high as the heavens are above the earth, so great is My love for you because you fear Me; as far as the east is from the west, so far have I removed your transgressions from you.

My precious child, call to Me, and I will answer you, and show you great and mighty things, which you do not know. Always pray to Me about your every concern, pray from your mouth and pray from your heart, I hear every thought that you think. Everything that you care about, I care about also because it concerns you. Cast all your cares and anxiety on Me because I love you. Trust in Me, the LORD YOUR GOD, with all your heart, do not depend on your own understanding; In everything acknowledge Me, And I will direct your paths. Do not worry about anything, but in everything big or small, by prayer, with thanksgiving, present your requests to Me, the Most High God. And I will give you My peace in your heart, peace that is beyond all human understanding, and it will guard your heart and your mind in Christ Jesus. Always be joyful. Keep on praying always. No matter what happens, always be thankful, for this is My will for you because you belong to Me.

My precious child, Study My Book of law and truth, the Holy Bible, do not let My words depart from your mouth; meditate on it day and night, so that you may be careful to do everything written in it. Then you will be prosperous and successful. My words are Spirit, and they are Life. If you remain in me and my words remain in you, ask whatever you will, and it will be given you. For the word of God is living and powerful. Sharper than any double-edged sword, it penetrates even to dividing soul and spirit, joints and marrow; it judges the thoughts and attitudes of the heart. The most important thing you will ever own is your Bible because it gives you knowledge of Me, The Most High God. It makes the poor rich, it gives hope to the hopeless, faith to the fearful, food to the hungry, water to the thirsty, love to the despised, comfort to the lonely, freedom to the prisoner, health to the sick, light in the darkness, and life to the dying.

My precious child I have set up circumstances and situations in your life to cause you to seek Me and find Me. I desire that you know Me. I am The Lord your God, full of compassion, and gracious, slow to anger, abounding in love and faithfulness. Let not the wise man glory in his wisdom, Let not the mighty man glory in his might, Nor let the rich man glory in his riches; But My precious child glory in this, That you understand and know Me, That I am the LORD, exercising compassion, lovingkindness, judgment, and righteousness in the earth. For in these I delight and take pleasure.

All things are created for My pleasure and My pleasure is to show forth loving compassion. I have compassion on the poor and needy, and I am a Father to the fatherless, I help them, and I defend them. Far below Me are the heavens and the earth, I stoop to look down, and I lift the poor from the dirt and the needy from the garbage dump and I set them among princes. My precious child I want you to do these things also, have compassion on the poor and needy and help them, this is what it means to know Me. For I am Love, and when you live in love, you live in Me, and I live in you. Loving compassion is good, and this is what I require from you, to do what is right, to love compassion, and to walk humbly with your God.

As a father has compassion on his children, so I your LORD have compassion on you because you fear Me; for I know how you were formed, I remember that you are dust. Forever and ever My love is with you because you fear Me, and My righteousness with your children's children; with those who keep My covenant and remember to obey My laws. My law is to love. You shall love the LORD your God with all your heart, with all your soul, and with all your mind. This is the first and great commandment. And the second is like it: You shall love your neighbor as yourself. On these two commandments all of My laws are based. When you walk in love you are obeying all My laws. When you walk in Love, you are walking in My Holy Spirit, for I AM LOVE!

My precious child come and live in My shelter, in the protection of the Most High God, you will find rest in the presence of the Almighty. You will say, "This I declare of the LORD: He alone is my refuge, my place of safety; he is my God, and I am trusting him." My precious child I will rescue you from every trap and protect you from the fatal plague. I will shield you with My wings. I will shelter you with My feathers. My faithful promises are your armor and protection. Do not be afraid of the terrors of the night, nor fear the dangers of the day, nor dread the plague that stalks in darkness, nor the disaster that strikes at midday. Though a thousand fall at your side, though ten thousand are dying around you, these evils will not touch you. But you will see it with your eyes; you will see how the wicked are punished.

Because you My precious child make the LORD your refuge, because you make the Most High your shelter, no evil will conquer you; no plague will come near your dwelling. For I order My angels to protect you wherever you go. They will hold you with their hands to keep you from striking your foot on a stone. You will trample down lions and poisonous snakes; you will crush fierce lions and serpents under your feet!

My precious child, My servant, and My friend, whom I have chosen, I have chosen you and have not rejected you. So do not fear, for I am with you; do not be dismayed, for I am your God. I will strengthen you and help you; I will hold you up with my righteous right hand. All who come against you will surely be ashamed and disgraced; those who oppose you will be as nothing and perish. Though you search for your enemies, you will not find them. Those who wage war against you will be as nothing at all. For I am the LORD, your God, who takes hold of your right hand and says to you, do not fear; I will help you. Do not be afraid, for I myself will help you declares the LORD, your Redeemer. You will rejoice in the LORD and glory in the Holy One of Israel.

My precious child, when you asked Me to forgive your sins and come into your heart I sent My Holy Spirit into you to comfort you, to give you power, and as proof to you that I have adopted you as My child. The Holy Spirit shall lead you into all truth because He shall testify of Jesus, and He will give you power to testify of Jesus. I will speak to you through My Holy Spirit that is in you, He will tell you what is right and wrong, what is love and hate. My Holy Spirit is a gentle whisper inside your heart telling you the path to walk in. If you walk in My Spirit you will walk in love, you will not sin. And you will see great and mighty things happen before you, they will not be accomplished by strength, nor by outside force, but by My Spirit says the LORD ALMIGHTY. Through My Holy Spirit I shall give you supernatural gifts that you may be blessed, and that you shall bless others through demonstrating My love for them. My Holy Spirit will be with you throughout your whole life, and after I will receive you into My glory.

I your LORD say to you I will rescue you because you love me. I will protect you because you trust in my name. When you call on me, I will answer; I will be with you in trouble. I will rescue you and honor you. I will satisfy you with a long life and give you my salvation. Call upon Me in the day of trouble; I will deliver you, and you shall glorify Me. It is your destiny.

Thus Says THE LORD Your GOD!

Father's Love Letter[7]

An intimate message from God to YOU.

What is Father's Love Letter?

Father's Love Letter is a compilation of paraphrased Bible verses from Genesis to Revelation that are presented in the form of a love letter from God to you. This simple message of love has been experienced by millions of people around the world in over 100 language translations and today, we want to share it with you.

INTRODUCTION:

The words you are about to experience are true. For they come from the very heart of God. He loves YOU. And He is the Father you have been looking for all your life. This is His love letter to you.

My Child,

You may not know me, but I know everything about you. (Psalm 139:1).
I know when you sit down and when you rise up. (Psalm 139:2).
I am familiar with all your ways. (Psalm 139:3).
Even the very hairs on your head are numbered. (Matthew 10:29-31).
For you were made in my image. (Genesis 1:27).
In me you live and move and have your being. (Acts 17:28).
For you are my offspring. (Acts 17:28).

---

[7] https://www.fathersloveletter.com/text.html. Father's Love Letter used by permission Father Heart Communications ©1999 FathersLoveLetter.com.

I knew you even before you were conceived. (Jeremiah 1:4-5).
I chose you when I planned creation. (Ephesians 1:11-12).
You were not a mistake, for all your days are written in my book. (Psalm 139:15-16).
I determined the exact time of your birth and where you would live. (Acts 17:26).
You are fearfully and wonderfully made. (Psalm 139:14).
I knit you together in your mother's womb. (Psalm 139:13).
And brought you forth on the day you were born. (Psalm 71:6).
I have been misrepresented by those who don't know me. (John 8:41-44).
I am not distant and angry, but am the complete expression of love. (1 John 4:16).
And it is my desire to lavish my love on you. (1 John 3:1).
Simply because you are my child, and I am your Father. (1 John 3:1).
I offer you more than your earthly father ever could. (Matthew 7:11).
For I am the perfect father. (Matthew 5:48).
Every good gift that you receive comes from my hand. (James 1:17).
For I am your provider and I meet all your needs. (Matthew 6:31-33).
My plan for your future has always been filled with hope. (Jeremiah 29:11).
Because I love you with an everlasting love. (Jeremiah 31:3).
My thoughts toward you are countless as the sand on the seashore. (Psalm 139:17-18).
And I rejoice over you with singing. (Zephaniah 3:17).
I will never stop doing good to you. (Jeremiah 32:40).
For you are my treasured possession. (Exodus 19:5).
I desire to establish you with all my heart and all my soul. (Jeremiah 32:41).
And I want to show you great and marvelous things. (Jeremiah 33:3).

If you seek me with all your heart, you will find me. (Deuteronomy 4:29).
Delight in me and I will give you the desires of your heart. (Psalm 37:4).
For it is I who gave you those desires. (Philippians 2:13).
I am able to do more for you than you could possibly imagine. (Ephesians 3:20).
For I am your greatest encourager. (2 Thessalonians 2:16-17).
I am also the Father who comforts you in all your troubles. (2 Corinthians 1:3-4).
When you are brokenhearted, I am close to you. (Psalm 34:18).
As a shepherd carries a lamb, I have carried you close to my heart. (Isaiah 40:11).
One day I will wipe away every tear from your eyes. (Revelation 21:3-4).
And I'll take away all the pain you have suffered on this earth. (Revelation 21:3-4).
I am your Father, and I love you even as I love my son, Jesus. (John 17:23).
For in Jesus, my love for you is revealed. (John 17:26).
He is the exact representation of my being. (Hebrews 1:3).
He came to demonstrate that I am for you, not against you. (Romans 8:31).
And to tell you that I am not counting your sins. (2 Corinthians 5:18-19).
Jesus died so that you and I could be reconciled. (2 Corinthians 5:18-19).
His death was the ultimate expression of my love for you. (1 John 4:10).
I gave up everything I loved that I might gain your love. (Romans 8:31-32).
If you receive the gift of my son Jesus, you receive me. (1 John 2:23).
And nothing will ever separate you from my love again. (Romans 8:38-39).

Come home and I'll throw the biggest party heaven has ever seen. (Luke 15:7).
I have always been Father, and will always be Father. (Ephesians 3:14-15).
My question is … Will you be my child? (John 1:12-13).
I am waiting for you. (Luke 15:11-32).
Love, Your Dad.

Almighty God.

A Love Letter To You From God[8]

To my precious child,

I want you to know something. I created you. I knew who you were, who you would become long before you were even born. I knew that you would grow up, that you would fall down, that sometimes you would question yourself even though you were made in my image and I love you so very much.

Some days are easier than others. Some days you pray to me with joy bubbling from your heart. I tell the sun to shine on your face and watch as you dance, laugh, kiss, feel free. In those moments, I know that you are living the way I intended — peacefully, abundantly, and in my light — and I try to show you how beautiful life can be.

But some days you get lost. The pain comes in waves and you suddenly forget who I am, how I have the power to rescue you from whatever demons you face. You turn away from me, try to take matters into your own hands. But you do not have to do that.

You do not ever have to feel like you are fighting alone.

I am here. I am always here. I watch you slip and lose your footing. I watch you turn to vices, chasing emptiness in people, in bottles, in bad habits, spinning yourself in circles. I reach out my hand to you, try to grab ahold of you, give you miracles and blessings and signs, but you do not see them.

You think I have abandoned you — but you are my creation — I will never leave you.

---

[8] By Marisa Donnelly, Updated October 25, 2019. https://thoughtcatalog.com/marisa-donnelly/2018/01/a-love-letter-to-you-from-god/

I know the number of hairs on your head, the way your mouth turns into a crooked grin when you laugh, the slight curve of your hips. I know the unpolished fingernails, the callouses, the muscles that fill your upper back.

I know how you loved that girl and are still heartbroken over her. I know how you gave your heart to that boy who ended up falling for someone else. I know what you think about when it's late and you can't fall asleep, the songs you sing in the shower, your favorite color, the meal you always cook when you're sick.

I know you try to fill yourself with all the temporary things of this world even though I gave my Son for you. It breaks my heart.

But I want you to know who I am; I do not want to force you to come to me. I want you to see the truths of my word in your life and know, beyond any doubt, that I am your God, and I will never forsake you.

I long to have a relationship with you. I crave closeness; I want you to be transparent with me and try, every day, to bring yourself and others to my light.

I want you to know that the only promise of forever comes from and through me. I want you to see the blessings I have given you; the beautiful ways life has fallen into place when you trust me and my plan. I want you to know that you will make mistakes, you will sin, you will hurt my heart over and over again.

But I will still love you.

I will never stop loving you. And as long as you seek forgiveness, as long as you repent, as long as you ask me to be in your heart and life and believe that my Son died for you

— I will forever be within you — guiding you, filling you, moving you forward in hope and joy.

My precious child, you are seen. Your prayers are heard. Your wishes and hopes and pains are felt. Sometimes I do not give you what you want because I am bringing you something better. Sometimes I do not answer you in the way you would like, but trust me anyways. I have a plan.

Do not wander this earth without a purpose; seek that within me and I will give it to you. Do not let yourself be beaten down or abused, turn to me for light. Do not tell yourself that you have to move through these days without anyone beside you because I am here.

You are my child, and nothing will change that.

Through whatever darkness or whatever storm, I love you. And you have nothing to fear.

Love,

Your Father.

Love Letter From God[9]

This love letter from God feels like a warm embrace from God. God speaks to you from his heart, to your heart, to reveal his deep love for you. Take time to read and re-read it, so these words from God's heart can sink deep into your own heart and bring deep healing and new strength.

The message you will read below, is a personal love letter from God, for you. God is pure love. He loves you with a love that cannot be described in normal words. He longs to show you how much He loves you, so you can find rest in His arms of compassion. Therefor He gave us the Holy Spirit, who gives us the gifts of the Spirit. These gifts of the Spirit make it possible for God to express His deep, passionate eternal love for us. The Bible speaks for example about the gift of prophecy, which makes it possible for Christians to become a vessel of the voice of God, so God can speak through them and touch the hearts of His beloved people in a very personal, direct way.

Here you can read such a prophetic word, inspired by the Holy Spirit, showing us how much God loves us. Thus, it is a true love letter from God.

These words have not been made up by me, but have truly been given by the Lord Himself, as the Bible says:

'Whoever speaks, is to do so as one who is speaking the utterances of God.' (1 Peter 4:11)

Please take a few minutes, to allow this love letter from God to sink deep into your heart.

---

[9] David Sorensen. https://www.godisreal.today/love-letter-god/

You have been created by love, to live in love and to share God's love. Love is the very reason of your existence. That is why it is so important that we get a deep and powerful revelation of the love of God.

Read and re-read this love letter from God, to give the words the chance to go beyond your mind and reach the depths of your heart… Then the truth will set you free.

My beloved,

So, you know that if I were with you in tangible form, I would take you in my arms and cherish you?

I would tell you how precious you are to Me.

I would tell you how beautiful you are.

I would tell you how much I love you.

You would see my eyes… You would hear the sound of my voice. You would feel how affected I am over you.

You would see that I am your Father. And your best Friend.

You would understand that I will never leave you, that I am always watching you, full of love.

I am here. Do not think that I am not there, my beloved. I am here.

If I could let you see how I feel about you, you would be surprised. No, astonished. You would not be able to believe it. You would say 'it is too beautiful, too loving, too great, this is too beautiful.'

Still it is the truth.

If I could make you look into my eyes, if I could let you see the way I look at you, you would be so liberated.

Do you realize that?

So much fear would disappear. Your heart would experience so much joy.

I am here my child. I am speaking to you right now.

I am here, my beloved and I am singing a song over you. To show you how precious you are to Me. To show you how beloved you are to Me. (YOU, yes, you.... Really you!)

If you could see how much joy the angels that are with Me have over you. If you could see how proud they are of you.

Because you fight for Me, to do my will despite the many stumblings you make sometimes. They are proud of you. Because they know how hard the battle sometimes is, they know how much the enemy wants to destroy you.

But they are fighting abreast with you and Me, says Jesus. They are fighting together with us to show you that there is a joy reserved for you, that there is a freedom I have in store for you.

Just trust Me. You can rest. You can relax.

Let your head rest in My loving hands. You have been striding so much, fighting so much, my child.

Just come and put your head in my loving arms in peace and surrender.

With Me you are safe, so safe, so safe, so safe.

I am here, says Jesus. I am here. I am holding on to you.

And I will give you the rest you need.

I am here. And I am always looking at you in everything you do. Full of love. Full of joy. Because I know you have entrusted your heart to Me.

Do not give up, my beloved. Take new courage. Do not be afraid of the future.

I am here. Really. I am here. And I am with you. Always.

Lots of love,

– Your heavenly Father and Jesus Christ, through the Holy Spirit.

Praying the Names and Attributes of God[10]

We have compiled 30 names and attributes of God with accompanying verses to help you learn more about Him and be drawn into worship. Use this guide to enrich your understanding of God by taking a description of Him and meditating on it, drawing you into worship throughout the day.

God is infinitely far above our ability to fully understand, He tells us through the Scriptures very specific truths about Himself so that we can know what He is like, and be drawn to worship Him. The following is a list of 30 names and attributes of God. Use this guide for 30 days to enrich your time set apart with God by taking one description of Him and meditating on that for one day, along with the accompanying passage. Worship God, focusing on Him and His character.

Day 1 - God is Jehovah. The name of the independent, self-complete being — "I AM WHO I AM" — only belongs to Jehovah God. Our proper response to Him is to fall down in fear and awe of the One who possesses all authority. — Exodus 3:13-15

Day 2 - God is Jehovah-M'Kaddesh. This name means "the God who sanctifies." A God separate from all that is evil requires that the people who follow Him be cleansed from all evil. — Leviticus 20:7,8

Day 3 - God is infinite. God is beyond measurement—we cannot define Him by proportions or magnitude. He has no beginning, no end, and no limits. — Romans 11:33

Day 4 - God is omnipotent. God is all-powerful. He spoke all things into being, and all things—every micro-organism, every

[10] The Navigators. https://www.navigators.org/resource/praying-names-attributes-god/

breath we take—are sustained by Him. There is nothing too difficult for Him to do. — Jeremiah 32:17,18; Jeremiah 32:26,27

Day 5 - God is good. God is the embodiment of perfect goodness. He is kind, caring, and full of favor toward all of creation. —Psalm 119:65-72.

Day 6 - God is love. God's love is so great that He gave His only Son to bring us into fellowship with Him. God's love not only encompasses the world, but also embraces each of us personally and intimately. — 1 John 4:7-10

Day 7 - God is Jehovah-Jireh. This name means "the God who provides." Just as He provided yesterday, He will also provide today and tomorrow. He grants deliverance from sin, the oil of joy for the ashes of sorrow, and eternal citizenship in His Kingdom for all those adopted into His household. — Genesis 22:9-14.

Day 8 - God is Jehovah-shalom. This name means "the God of peace." We are meant to know the fullness of God's perfect peace, or His "shalom." God's peace surpasses understanding and sustains us even through difficult times. It is the product of fully being what we were created to be. — Judges 6:16-24.

Day 9 - God is immutable. All that God is, He has always been. All that He has been and is, He will ever be. He is ever perfect and unchanging. — Psalm 102:25-28

Day 10 - God is transcendent. God is not merely eminent, the highest being. He is transcendent—existing beyond and above the created universe. — Psalm 113:4,5.

Day 11 - God is just. God is righteous and holy, fair, and equitable in all things. We can trust Him to always do what is right. — Psalm 75:1-7.

Day 12 - God is holy. God's holiness is not simply our best image of perfection. God is utterly and supremely untainted. His holiness stands apart—unique and incomprehensible. — Revelation 4:8-11.

Day 13 - God is Jehovah-rophe. This name means "Jehovah heals." God alone provides the remedy for mankind's brokenness through His son, Jesus Christ. The Gospel is the physical, moral, and spiritual remedy for all people. — Exodus 15:22-26.

Day 14 - God is self-sufficient. All things are God's to give, and all that is given is given by Him. Everything we give Him was initially given to us by Him. — Acts 17:24-28.

Day 15 - God is omniscient. This means God is all-knowing. God's knowledge encompasses every possible piece of information regarding anything that currently exists, existed in the past, or will exist in the future. — Psalm 139:1-6.

Day 16 - God is omnipresent. God is everywhere—in and around everything, close to everyone. "'Do not I fill heaven and earth?' declares the Lord." — Psalm 139:7-12.

Day 17 - God is merciful. God's merciful compassion is never ending and does not run dry. Through His provision in Christ, He took the judgment that was rightfully ours and placed it on His own shoulders. He waits and works now for all people to turn to Him and to live under His justification. — Deuteronomy 4:29-31.

Day 18 - God is sovereign. God presides over every event, great or small, and He is in control of our lives. He rules all creation with all knowledge and power. - — 1 Chronicles 29:11-13.

Day 19 - God is Jehovah-Nissi. This name means "God our banner." Under His banner we go from triumph to triumph and say, “Thanks be to God, who gives us the victory through our Lord Jesus Christ” (1 Corinthians 15:57). — Exodus 17:8-15.

Day 20 - God is wise. God knows and acts with perfect wisdom in all things. He always acts for our good, which is to conform us to Christ. — Proverbs 3:19,20.

Day 21 - God is faithful. Out of His faithfulness God honors His covenants and fulfills His promises. Our hope for the future rests upon God’s faithfulness. — Psalm 89:1-8.

Day 22 - God is wrathful. Unlike human anger, God’s wrath is never capricious, self-indulgent, or irritable. It is the right and necessary reaction to objective moral evil. — Nahum 1:2-8.

Day 23 - God is full of grace. Grace is God’s good pleasure that moves Him to grant value where it is undeserved and to forgive debt that cannot be repaid. — Ephesians 1:5-8.

Day 24 - God is our Comforter. Jesus called the Holy Spirit the “Comforter,” and the apostle Paul writes that the Lord is “the God of all comfort.” — 2 Corinthians 1:3,4.

Day 25 - God is El-Shaddai. This name means “God Almighty,” the God who is all-sufficient and all-bountiful, the source of all blessings. — Genesis 49:22-26.

Day 26 - God is Father. Jesus taught us to pray, “Our Father” (Matthew 6:9), and the Spirit of God taught us to cry, “Abba, Father.,” an intimate Aramaic term similar to “Daddy.” The Creator of the universe cares for each one of us as if we were the only child He had. — Romans 8:15-17.

Day 27 - God is the Church’s head. God the Son, Jesus, is the head of the Church. As the head, the part of the body that sees, hears, thinks, and decides, He gives the orders that the rest of the body lives by. — Ephesians 1:22,23.

Day 28 - God is our intercessor. Knowing our temptations, God the Son intercedes for us. He opens the doors for us to boldly ask God the Father for mercy. Thus, God is both the initiation and conclusion of true prayer. — Hebrews 4:14-16.

Day 29 - God is Adonai. This name means “Master” or “Lord.” God, our Adonai, calls all God’s people to acknowledge themselves as His servants, claiming His right to reign as Lord of our lives. — 2 Samuel 7:18-20.

Day 30 - God is Elohim. This name means “Strength” or “Power.” He is transcendent, mighty, and strong. Elohim is the great name of God, displaying His supreme power, sovereignty, and faithfulness in His covenant relationship with us. — Genesis 17:7,8.

Sources: The Knowledge of the Holy, by A.W. Tozer; Names of God, by Nathan Stone; and God of Glory, by Kenneth Landon.

Appendices

How To Begin Your Journey With God

John 14:6, NIV - *Jesus answered, "I am the way and the truth and the life. No one comes to the Father except through me.*

Living a life in partnership with God, through His Son Jesus, is the greatest adventure any person can ever experience. How can we make the initial decision to trust Him with our whole life, and begin to live for Him? It is as easy as A-B-C-D!

A – Admit that Jesus is indeed the only way to salvation, and that our hearts are completely lost without Him. (Romans 3:23, Romans 3:10).

B – Believe that Jesus died on the cross for our sins and rose from the dead for our freedom. (John 1:29, John 3:16-18, Acts 4:12).

C – Confess Jesus as our personal Lord and Saviour, the new leader of our lives. (Romans 10:9, John 5:24, John 1:12-13).

D – Decide to follow Jesus daily, and do what He asks of us. (Luke 9:23-24).

PRAYER

We can make those four choices, by saying a prayer something like this:

Jesus, I realize that I am lost without You, and You are the only way that I can experience freedom.

Thank You for dying on the cross to save me from the penalty of sin, and for rising from the dead so that I could be completely free.

I choose to confess and put my trust in You as my Lord and Savior. I give my whole heart and my whole life to You.

I ask You to indwell me by Your Holy Spirit, so that I can have Your help to do my best to follow You and please You each and every day.

In Jesus' name I pray. Amen!

Who Is David R. Hibbert?

David R. Hibbert grew up on the edge of a farm in rural Ontario, just north of London. After graduating from the University of Western Ontario, he worked as an Electrical-Mechanical Maintenance and Design Engineer in Hamilton, Ontario, before accepting the call to full-time Christian ministry.

During Bible school training in Peterborough, Ontario, he spent his summers as an interim Pastor in Northern Ontario. Upon graduation, he served as the Director of a Men's Mission for two years.

Then, at the leading of the Holy Spirit, he moved to the South Shore of Montreal, Quebec, Canada to plant a church and develop an Apostolic Centre.

He enjoys teaching, exhortation, short-term missions and developing training courses, books, and manuals. His Mission Statement is "to build, equip, and release purpose in people's lives."

He is married to an incredible woman named Kathleen, and has four grown awesome children – Kristen, Thomas, Kaylea and Elissa – as well as a growing number of grandchildren.

Other Books And Courses By David R. Hibbert

Note: These books are available around the world as paperbacks through Amazon, and as eBooks through Amazon and www.DestinyResource.ca.

Answering The BIG Questions

Every few years it is good to check our foundations, to see if there are any cracks in them, or if they have shifted because of the pressures of life.

"Answering The BIG Questions" is a new and fresh look at the really BIG questions of life, to ensure that our lives are still built on a good foundation. We look at God's Original Purpose, Understanding What We Lost, Understanding What We Really Need, Understanding How The Spirit Conforms Us, Understanding Our New Identity, and Understanding How To Live in Victory. A refreshing and liberating study of how to live as a child of God.

Building An Apostolic Centre

In this book we will develop an understanding of what an Apostolic Centre is, how the early church grew because of Apostolic Centres, and what are the basic ingredients that are necessary to ensure the establishment of a healthy Apostolic Centre that will bless the region and advance the Kingdom of God within that region.

Christmas Quizzicles

This eBook is a collection of some quizzes, games, stories, and inspirational notes – some serious, some thought-provoking, and some just plain silly. They are just a sampling of the many that I have collected over the years ... fun resources for children of all ages. May you enjoy them as much I have enjoyed collecting them.

These quizzes are great for family gatherings, small groups, church parties and more. Simply copy, hand out, and let the fun begin. Now have fun and celebrate!

Developing An Intentional Culture For Your Church, Business Or Family – Determining Your Relational Atmosphere

A culture is the relational atmosphere that every organization must have, in order to be healthy and effective. In this book David Hibbert explains the critical importance of planning, documenting, and promoting the desired culture. Although this book is written primarily for church communities, it applies equally as well to any group where people must work and co-exist together.

Discovering Your P.U.R.P.O.S.E.: Volume I – Developing A Personal Mission Statement

You have a purpose, a destiny, a special assignment from God Himself! And when you discover that purpose, commit to that purpose, and make decisions in alignment with that purpose, the Creator of the universe ensures that all of the resources in heaven and earth are directed toward you, so that you can fulfill that purpose.

There are seven primary indicators that God has given you, to help you discover what is your purpose in life. In Volume One of "Discovering Your P.U.R.P.O.S.E.", you will be taught the first two indicators to discover what is your purpose, and then be guided, step by step, to developing your own personal Mission Statement for your life, that you can use to help you stay on track, and make the best decisions for your life's purpose.

This Book can change the direction and focus of your life!

Discovering Your P.U.R.P.O.S.E.: Volume II – Realizing Your Specific Assignment

You have a purpose, a destiny, a special assignment from God Himself! And when you discover that purpose, commit to that purpose, and make decisions in alignment with that purpose, the Creator of the universe ensures that all of the resources in heaven and earth are directed toward you, so that you can fulfill that purpose.

There are seven primary indicators that God has given you, to help you discover what is your purpose in life. In Volume Two of "Discovering Your P.U.R.P.O.S.E.", you will discover your Reoccurring Experiences, Personality Traits, Overriding Motivations, Spiritual Gifts and Extra Resources that you have, that will help you to fine-tune your purpose into a specific area of God-given assignment.

This Book can change the direction and focus of your life!

Drawing Close To God In A Time Of Crisis (Finding God in the Storm).

In this book, filled with much encouragement and Biblical insight, David Hibbert shares a simple and practical strategy for helping us draw closer to God, no matter what is going on around us. Embrace the tools and learn from the examples of how you can draw close to God in any crisis.

Embracing The Fivefold Ministry – Volume I – Introduction To The Fivefold Ministry

In this introduction to the fivefold ministry, you will discover the purpose of the fivefold ministries, their differences, how they work together in a church service, what happens when a church is only one-fold or two-fold, and church government in a fivefold church.

Embracing The Fivefold Ministry – Volume II – Understanding The Apostolic Ministry

Coming soon!

Embracing The Fivefold Ministry – Volume III – Understanding The Prophetic Ministry

Coming soon!

Experience Resurrection Power: By Embracing The Cross

In this Book, David Hibbert looks at the three parts of the cross; the vertical board, the horizontal board, and the foot of the cross, to explain the three most important things that Jesus did on the cross for us. He also shares a little understood consequence of Jesus' work on the cross that is indispensable to embrace, if we are going to truly experience Christian maturity in our lives. He clearly describes what must happen when we come to the cross if we want resurrection power in our lives. He also shares an amazing fact about an overlooked Christian ordinance that was designed by God to give us a special impartation of grace for experiencing resurrection power.

Fasting Made (Super) Simple

Biblical fasting has been very much misunderstood by many, if not most people. Because of that, for those who have tried to fast, and seen minimal or no results, it has left a poor impression on them. In this eBook you will be given very simple step-by-step and practical information on how anyone can fast, as well as the hidden key to fasting that will unlock its power for your life. Get ready for breakthrough!

F.E.A.R.L.E.S.S. – Eight Keys To Overcoming Fear

Fear is one of humankind's greatest enemies. At the least, it hinders and limits us. At the most, it keeps us in bondage, and plays havoc on our health, our relationships, and our potential. In this book David Hibbert gives you 8 keys to help you overcome every fear in your life.

Feasting On Christ's Grace At His Table

God has lovingly provided for His children, many sources of His amazing grace. Come and understand, and receive, the incredible grace of God that is available to each one of us, when we recognize it, and learn how to receive it, through the celebration of the Lord's Supper, also known as the Lord's Table, or Communion.

Five Keys For Effective Prayer Evangelism

In this book, David Hibbert shares with the reader five rarely used keys for praying for those who do not yet know Christ, or who have wandered away from faith in Christ. The task of bringing people to

Christ is not just about preaching the gospel, it is also about waging spiritual warfare against Satan's tactics that affect a person's mind and heart and spiritual sight. Apply these five Biblical keys and see your prayer effectiveness reach a whole new level!

Forgiveness – The Key To Freedom

Forgiveness is such a really big deal! So many people struggle with unforgiveness, resentment, and personal wounds caused by others. And it is keeping so many people sick, limited, bound up, and side-tracked. God wants us to be free. Jesus died so that we can be free. But until we learn how to forgive, and live a life of forgiveness towards others, we will never be free.

This book looks at the topic of forgiveness … what it is, what is isn't, why is it difficult to forgive, why we need to forgive, Biblical mindsets that help us forgive, and how we can truly forgive, so that we can be completely free in our lives.

Healing Father Wounds

Most Christians today have so much knowledge about Jesus, and yet we tend to be ineffective and unproductive. Why is this so? Because we are lacking certain qualities in our lives, because of father wounds. So, we need to have our father wounds healed, so that our knowledge can be translated into effectiveness.

In this book, you will discover what father wounds are, how you received your father wounds, how they affect your life, and God's amazing plan to re-parent you, so that you can be healed from all of your father wounds, and become the effective son or daughter of God that you were created to be.

Healing It's Yours

In this book David Hibbert uses much Biblical support to tackle the question, "It is always God's will to heal?" He then challenges us to consider that we may the solution to our own healing. Next, he presents many practical scriptures and examples to understand both keys to healing, and how to keep your healing. A very practical and Biblical explanation of healing for today.

How To Experience True Freedom

God wants us to become totally free. He wants us to experience the fullness of His forgiveness today, and He wants us to be free so that we do not repeat the cycle of failure in our lives.

This book will give you the understanding and tools you need to experience true freedom in your life. Experience true freedom from all guilt and shame and remorse, as well as damaged emotions from the offenses of others.

How To Gather Purposefully

When Christians meet together on a Sunday, why are they meeting? What is their goal? What do they expect to accomplish? Does God have any expectations from them?

This message will help Christians to understand how to meet with purpose and intention, so that God is truly glorified, His will is accomplished, and people are blessed by God as they meet. This message is very encouraging, practical, and brings much clarity to the gather of the local church.

How To Have A Healing Ministry

God wants every believer in Christ to share the love of Christ, minister to those who are suffering, and invite people into the Kingdom of God. The ministry of healing is a powerful tool to open hearts to the gospel. In this teaching, David Hibbert details ten keys that are necessary for anyone wanting to have a sustainable healing ministry. He also shares a proven ten step checklist for connecting with the sick, receiving permission to pray for them, and maximizing healing results. Very insightful, practical, and challenging.

How To Hear God's Voice – Five Keys For Clarity

Every Christian wants to know God's will, but to know the fullness of God's will, we need to be able to hear His voice.

In this book, you will be given a simple, yet highly effective strategy for hearing God's voice. You will be amazed at how easy it is for you to hear God's voice. And you will be motivated to begin a life-long journey in daily hearing His voice and live in a new level of effectiveness in your walk with God.

How To Intercede For Your City

If we are a Christian, each one of us has a divine mandate to bring the gospel to our city. But we are often unsure what to do, how to do it, and how to be effective in doing it.

In this book you will learn how to intercede for your city, in a way, that you will actually see some results. This book is very practical, and includes information on the Biblical definition of nations, recent data on unreached and unengaged people groups, and statistics on migration from rural to city.

How To Self-Publish An eBook In Canada

For all of the aspiring authors out there, here is a very clear and simple explanation of the steps necessary to self-publish an eBook in Canada. Included in this book is information on the types, categories and main formats of eBooks, guidance on how to write an eBook, obtaining an ISBN number, opening an Amazon Kindle Direct Publishing Account, preparing, and publishing your eBook, and more.

Keys To Intimacy – Experiencing The Heart Of God

There is no trust without intimacy. Intimacy builds trust. In this series you will learn eight simple keys that will enable you to deepen your relationship with the lover of your soul and come to trust Him in a whole new way.

Learning How To Love: Manifesting Agape

Most of us still experience conflicts and offenses and damaged relationships. If love truly is as powerful a force as we say it is, then we must be willing to ask a very serious question: "Do we really know how to love?" This book examines the different types of love, gives a thorough description of the highest form of love, and then presents simple strategies to develop the skills necessary to express this amazing love – God's love.

Making The Most Of The Christmas Season: Inspiration For A Great Christmas And An Awesome New Year

Christmas can be a CRAZY time. Planning for family gatherings, getting presents for those we love, reconnecting with friends, navigating through Christmas and Boxing Day (now boxing week) sales, and not to mention the dreaded "year-end" inventory lists and financial statements. What on earth happened to "Merry Christmas and a Happy New Year"?

In this book, the reader will be presented with five strategies to make Christmas both meaningful and enjoyable and be able to face the New Year with hope and expectation. In all, these five strategic attitudes are easily implemented, and can make the difference between year-end panic, and year end hope for an even better year ahead.

Natural Discipleship

We are first and foremost children of God, and we become children of God the moment we become a Christian, and we are immediately placed into the family of God. So, what if our growth to maturity is not agreement to a list of doctrinal statements, and a development of good Christian habits? What if our spiritual growth as Christians actually follows the same process as the natural growth of children into adulthood.

This book will show you how the best way to mature in Christ, is to follow the same five steps as natural growth of every child into adulthood.

No Fear – Choose Peace And Grow Stronger In A Time Of Crisis

In this book, published during the COVID-19 pandemic of 2020, David Hibbert presents a Christian perspective on crisis, and then shares a number of important principles on how to face a crisis as a

Christian, including how to do spiritual warfare during a crisis, how to pursue and fulfill your God-given purpose during a crisis, how to grow spiritually during a time of crisis, and how to stay in the peace of God during a crisis. This book will give you very practical tools so that you can go through the storm and come out even stronger.

Overcoming Fear In A Time Of Crisis – 28 Truths To Exchange Fear For Peace

This book was birthed in the middle of the COVID-19 pandemic of 2020, but the truths in it can equally apply to any pandemic or crisis in our lives. God's Word is applicable to every situation, and so this book will help you whether you are facing another world-wide epidemic, or a more focused personal crisis.

Read each chapter, consider it, meditate on it, and be encouraged. God is with you in your storm, and He will bring you to the other side!

Overcoming Self-Deception

When I first became a Christian, it seemed like everyone I met was concerned about doctrinal error. Do we believe the right things about the doctrine of the Holy Spirit, do we believe the right things about salvation, do we believe the right things about Jesus, do we believe the right things about the end times? In those early days, most error seemed to revolve around our interpretation of the scriptures. Today, however, much of the error that I have come across is not due to our interpretation of the scriptures, but due to our philosophy of how we even approach the Scriptures.

In this short book, I will look at what I believe is one of the most widespread errors in the church today, and then present a principle that will bring balance back to this error, as well as serve as a tool to avoid other errors in the future.

Overcoming The Orphan Stronghold

We believe that every Christian wants to be "fully conformed to the image of Christ" – they want to become all that they were created to be, and to fulfill their destiny here on earth.

However, every person on earth, including Christians, struggles with the orphan stronghold. It affects our faith in God, our ability to trust God, our ability to trust people, our ability to relate with others, our ability to have healthy marriages, our freedom in Christ, our healing, and even our destiny.

In these lessons, you will learn what the Orphan Stronghold is, where it came from, how it operates, how it manifests in us, and how we can begin to overcome it. God wants us free to be fully alive in Him!

Pulling Lessons From My Garden (Making Room For Abundant Life) – Kathleen R. Hibbert.

In this very humorous and insightful book, Kathy Hibbert compares our hearts to a garden (God did it first), and by examining the weeds that grow in her lawn and garden, she learns a number of lessons and discovers a number of keys that are necessary to eliminate (or at least minimize) the weeds that try to grow in our hearts.

Receiving The Seven-Fold Spirit Of God

In this book you will discover why most people, including many in the Pentecostal and Charismatic theological streams, have missed the full benefits of Pentecost. You will also discover what is the Seven-Fold Spirit of God, and how to embrace the fullness of the Holy Spirit. Get ready for breakthrough!

Seven Keys To Maturity In Christ

Most Christians want to grow in Christ, and to become mature Christians. But how is that accomplished? In this book we present seven keys that you can use to jump-start, and even quicken your Christian growth, as well as guarantee continued growth for the rest of your life. Learn how to apply the Keys of Liberty, Conformity, Identity, Authority, Clarity, Community, and Intimacy and discover the joy of maturity in Christ.

The Blessing Of Personal Prophecy

In this book, David Hibbert defines prophecy, public prophecy, and personal prophecy, and then validates Biblically that God uses people to minister personal prophecy today. Finally, he gives very practical guidelines for receiving, understanding, and responding to a personal prophetic word.

This book will answer the questions: What is Prophecy? Is Prophecy Still Valid Today? What Is The Purpose Of Prophecy? Our Response To Prophecy. How To Maximize The Blessing Of Your Prophecy. What Should Be Our Response To Prophecy? How To Maximize The Blessing Of Your Prophecy.

The Call To Manhood (Choosing To Become A Man).

The world desperately needs REAL Men. And men desperately need to learn how to step up into Manhood. This book can be used for personal use, for men's Bible studies, or even for men's retreats. In it you will be given vision and practical tools to help you respond to the call to manhood and step up as a man.

The Five Seasons Of Marriage (Growing A Marriage That Lasts A Lifetime).

The Seasons Of Marriage are predictable and necessary stages involving the physical, emotional, mental, relational, and spiritual areas of life. Through them, partners journey toward the lifetime goal of growth as individuals and as a couple.

This book will give you the information you need to understand why your marriage may be struggling, and the tools you need to bring your marriage back to health, so that it grow into a fulfilling lifetime adventure.

The Four Pillars Of Christian Maturity

In this book, David Hibbert looks at the Four Pillars Of Christian Maturity, as outlined in Acts 2:42-47. He explains each of the four pillars, and then gives practical examples of why they are so important to our spiritual health and maturity. He also gives a graphic example of what will happen to our spiritual life if we neglect these four pillars.

The Power of a Blessing

Every human being longs for love, longs for acceptance, longs for the knowledge that they are valued by someone, and that they have a purpose worth living for. God has given us the principle of blessing as a way to deposit within a person's heart, the assurance of all of these things. Learn how to transform a person's life for greatness, with your words and actions, in this simple five-part Biblical principle.

The Search For A Father: The Story Of David

In this insightful book, you will experience an intimate examination of David's search for a father, from his infancy, as a teen, and into his adult years. You will discover the cause of much of his failure, the source of much of his pain, and the secret of his later years of success. And you will conclude that he found what we all need, the presence of a godly father.

When Christians Face Crises

Why did this happen? Why did God allow it? Does God really care? These are some of the many questions that are asked "When Christians Face Crises". This book is not about religious platitudes are simplistic arguments. Instead, the writer seeks to give clear, Biblical answers to our very difficult questions concerning pain and suffering. This book will give the reader a compassionate and Biblical perspective on suffering and inspire hope to those presently in the midst of a crisis.

Made in the USA
Columbia, SC
27 June 2023